ANNE BRONTË REIMAGINED

ANNE BRONTË REIMAGINED

A VIEW FROM THE TWENTY-FIRST CENTURY

ADELLE HAY

Saraband

Published by Saraband
Digital World Centre
1 Lowry Plaza, The Quays
Salford M50 3UB
www.saraband.net

ISBN: 9781912235643
ebook: 9781912235650

Printed and bound in Great Britain by Clays Ltd, Elcograf S.p.A.

FSC www.fsc.org MIX Paper from responsible sources FSC® C018072

10 9 8 7 6 5 4 3 2 1

Victorian novels were commonly printed with illustrations depicting scenes in the narrative. Accordingly, we've embellished this book with period images to emulate early editions of Brontë works. The illustrations reproduced in this book are from the author's collection, Saraband Image Library, or are sourced from shared-resource and public domain collections.

CONTENTS

This book is dedicated to

Jonathan, Edward and Evelyn.

INTRODUCTION

Anne Brontë was a pioneering female author. She began writing in her childhood in the 1820s, cultivating a literary habit that lasted her whole life. Her second and most famous work, *The Tenant of Wildfell Hall*, was groundbreaking in its choice of subject matter. She covered topics considered sensitive at the time, such as marital abuse, gender equality and how this should affect education, and married women's rights in an era when married women were viewed as the property of their husband. Anne Brontë was subsequently regarded as crude and coarse by most contemporary reviewers. This did not prevent the book from selling well during Anne's lifetime, however.

This is how I wish all biographical introductions about Anne Brontë would begin – acknowledging her successes and her strong sense of justice rather than her perceived weaknesses, and without having to compare her to her sisters, Charlotte and Emily. Ever since the publication of Elizabeth Gaskell's *The Life of Charlotte Brontë* (1857), there has been a tradition of describing Anne as quiet, 'meek and mild', the most physically frail of the Brontës. These words aren't bad in themselves but reading something on Anne Brontë full of descriptions like this – usually after a section where praise is heaped on her sisters – makes them feel derogatory and patronising.

Inevitably, Anne's writing is also compared to that of her sisters. Of course, there's nothing wrong with this – Charlotte, Emily and Anne (along with their brother, Branwell) were writing together from childhood and there's much to be learned by looking at how they worked together and inspired each other. But, unfortunately for Anne, her writing has often been compared harshly (I believe unnecessarily so) with that of Charlotte and Emily, and a common theme is to describe Anne's work as a way of measuring her sisters' genius.

In 1993, Muriel Spark wrote, 'I think her works are not good enough to be considered in any serious context of the nineteenth-century novel or that there exists any literary basis for comparison with the brilliant creative works of Charlotte and Emily… She was a writer who could "pen" a story well enough; she was a literary equivalent of a decent water-colourist.'

Interestingly, Muriel Spark originally had a very different opinion of Anne – in the 1950s she published articles on Anne's poetry and novels, but chose to omit all of her work on Anne in her later essay collections, writing, 'I do not now agree with my former opinion of Anne Brontë's value as a writer.'[1] So what changed?

Anne's literary and personal reputations have changed drastically since she was first published in 1846, in a volume of poetry along with her sisters. That book, published under the pseudonyms of Currer, Ellis and Acton Bell, went largely unnoticed, with a few positive reviews mostly focusing on Ellis's (Emily's) poems. But by the time Anne's first novel, *Agnes Grey*, was published in 1847, Charlotte's *Jane Eyre* was already a sensation. *Agnes Grey*, featuring a governess protagonist, was assumed by some to be a naïve first attempt by Currer Bell (Charlotte).[2]

Some reviews for *Agnes Grey* were quietly positive, whilst others criticised the author's vulgarity or compared the work unfavourably with the novels by the other Bells. *The Tenant of Wildfell Hall* (1848) received even more negative reviews addressing the crudeness of the subject matter, but this seemed to make it even more popular. The book sold incredibly well, despite accusations that it was 'coarse' and 'brutal'.[3]

After Anne's death, Charlotte suppressed any further republication of *The Tenant of Wildfell Hall*. This is discussed in more detail in Chapter Three, but one of the results of this was that Anne's reputation changed from vulgar to overly moralising, based on *Agnes Grey* and her religious poetry (some of which was heavily edited by Charlotte). Over the next century, an image emerged of Anne as pious and reserved, and it has been prevalent ever since. Despite the initial popularity of Anne's novels, she has been referred to as 'the other Brontë' and, more detrimentally, 'the boring Brontë'. It's an attitude that has survived into the twenty-first century and, unfortunately for me, I fell into the trap of believing these ideas of Anne for a long time.

I first encountered the Brontës aged twelve, when I visited the Brontë Parsonage Museum in Haworth, Yorkshire. I was entranced by their writing desks and their tiny books. An enthusiastic member of staff told me about how the young Brontës made the miniature books themselves and wrote fantastic stories in them in minuscule handwriting. The tiny writing, she said, served two purposes: to resemble print, and to make sure their father wouldn't be able to read it with his poor eyesight. The 170-year gap between us was immediately closed – as a young teenager I would also write strange stories and keep my journals in a code so that my parents couldn't read them. The Brontës were immediately real to me in a way that I hadn't expected them to be, and from that point on they have always been part of my life.

I am not alone with this fascination either, as the thousands of visitors to the parsonage every year demonstrates. As the writer Lucasta Miller has said, the Brontës 'have become mythic figures in their own right'. Anne's part in the Brontë myth is, as she puts it, to be 'regarded as very much the least interesting sister, mentioned, it seems, merely to make up the number three'.[4]

The first time I read *The Tenant of Wildfell Hall*, I was blown away by Anne's treatment of women's rights issues that are still prevalent today. I subsequently read *Agnes Grey* and could not believe these were written by the same Anne I had read about in biographies and on the internet, and the Anne that had been presented to me in popular culture. I immediately read everything I could about Anne, learning about her changing reputations and wondering which Anne was real and which was imaginary. Who is responsible for imagining her? Why has opinion of her changed so much, and how is it that she is still considered to be the boring Brontë?

There have been many biographies of the Brontës, with new biographical material emerging almost every year since the publication of Mrs Gaskell's *The Life of Charlotte Brontë*. Juliet Barker's outstanding biography of the whole family, *The Brontës* (1994), is an almost encyclopaedic account of the life of the family. In the last ten years, two fantastic biographies of Anne have been published: Nick Holland's *In Search of Anne Brontë* (2016) and Samantha Ellis's *Take Courage: Anne Brontë and the Art of Life* (2017). These have built on the work done by Winifred Gérin and Edward Chitham. Gérin's was one of the first sympathetic biographies of Anne, and Edward Chitham has done a lot to restore opinion of Anne's character and her literary reputation (all these biographies are discussed further in Chapter Three).

My aim, therefore, is not to recreate an account of the life of Anne Brontë, but to try to dispel some of the myths surrounding her while demonstrating how her work is more relevant than ever in the twenty-first century. I want to show that writing about religion doesn't mean that you can't employ humour – Anne was *funny*. She was observant, empathetic and able to weave her own experiences into a fictional narrative in a way that enhanced the characters and storyline.

Chapter One provides a snapshot overview of Anne's life that I hope provides the reader with a foundation and context for her works. We don't have much information from Anne herself (only five of her letters and two Diary Papers written by her remain), but letters from others to Anne, and anecdotes from those close to her, can give us clues about the real Anne Brontë.

Chapter Two is dedicated to Anne as a writer and later as the author Acton Bell. None of Anne's earliest prose survives, but we have poems, letters and Diary Papers to help us build a picture of her and what she was interested in writing. (The Brontës' spelling and punctuation was often very messy in their diaries and letters, especially those written when they were younger. Where they are quoted in this book, they have been corrected to make them easier to read, but it's important to remember that their writing wasn't perfect from the beginning – they worked hard to achieve their later standards.)

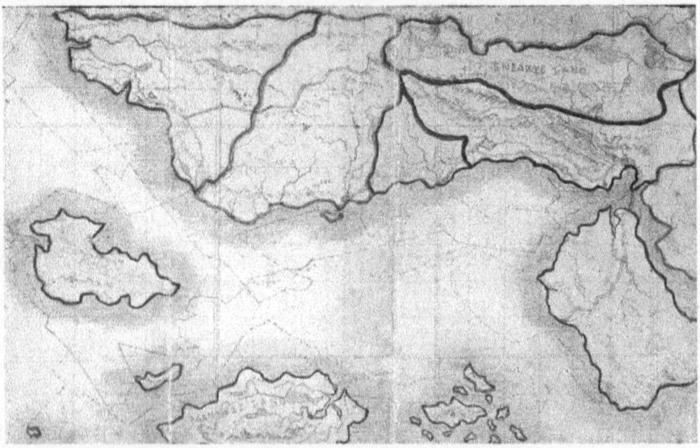

Branwell's map of the imaginary country of Angria, the scene of some of the young siblings' role-playing games (see Chapter One).

Anne also had a very personal attachment to poetry, both the reading and the writing of it. Her description of poems in *Agnes Grey* as 'pillars of witness' to a life lived has become central to understanding Anne's poetry. There is a danger here, however, of reading her works as almost completely autobiographical. How much of Anne's works can we assume came from her own experience? I hope to show that she was incredibly skilled at combining personal experience with imagination.

Chapter Three addresses how and why Anne's reputation has shifted so dramatically since her death. From Charlotte's take on 'Acton Bell' through to the most recent biographies, there have been many factors that contributed to how we see Anne. How has interest in Anne changed in the last sixty years, since Winifred Gérin's game-changing biography? Why is Anne experiencing a resurgence in popularity now, and how are recent portrayals of her, like in the 2016 biopic *To Walk Invisible*, changing to match changing attitudes?

Chapter Four explores Anne's relationship with nature. It's widely known that all the Brontës loved their rural home and the moors surrounding it; both Anne and Emily based their imaginary world of Gondal on the northern landscape around Haworth, and this is reflected in their poetry. Anne was also very sympathetic to the treatment of animals. Pets were a large part of life at the parsonage, and Anne's dog Flossy makes many appearances in Diary Papers and letters to friends and family – she was even the subject of a couple of portraits. Visiting Scarborough also instilled in Anne a love of the sea, which makes an appearance in some of the most romantic scenes in her novels.

Chapter Five is an investigation into how Anne has survived in the popular imagination as a frail and pious individual, seemingly welcoming of death. All the Brontës addressed religion in their works, in very different ways. This is perhaps unsurprising given that their father, Patrick, was a member of the clergy within the Church of England. This meant that religion and theology would have played a larger part in their lives than would have been the case for most people. But there were unique elements in Anne's life that affected her religious attitudes. How did her Aunt Branwell's early influence, for example, affect Anne's religious beliefs? How did Anne's religious crisis while at school affect her writing?

Agnes Grey is very critical of some aspects of the church and the clergy and it features Anne's quite radical reviews of religion. She was almost overstepping patriarchal boundaries in the treatment of religion in her novels – theology was the domain of men. Her father published moral stories and sermons himself, very different in tone to Anne's works, but it was not expected that women at the time would write such things. Religion is not as pervasive now as it was in the Brontës' day, and Anne's beliefs were relatively modern: her ideas about Universal Salvation and a loving and forgiving God are much closer in tone to more recent representations of religion than they were to the traditional beliefs of the nineteenth century that Anne struggled with.

Chapter Six looks at how Anne's ideas about social and moral reform are still relevant today. Almost 150 years after the publication of *The Tenant of Wildfell Hall*, emotional abuse in relationships and the power imbalance between men and women are still problematic. Anne's desire to do some good in the world took the form of using her skills as a writer to inform her readers about the truth as she saw it; her views on education, religion and women's rights were all present in both *Agnes Grey* and *The Tenant of Wildfell Hall*.

It is tempting to read all of the Brontës' works as semi-autobiographical. But that interpretation means you'd sometimes have to disregard the realities of the sisters' own experiences. A popular question is, 'How could they write about such passionate love if they never truly experienced it themselves?' Charlotte, we know, experienced an intense unrequited love for her teacher Constantin Héger, but even before this encounter she was writing about ardent love affairs in her earlier work. When considering where the Brontës got their ideas from, it would be foolish to ignore their reading habits and tastes – they were voracious readers from a young age and had access to a very unconventional library for such a young family. In Chapter Seven I have presented a list of books to read if you want a better understanding of their reading influences. From Bewick's *A History of British Birds* to Byron's epic *Don Juan*, it's easy to see how the books they read would have had a huge effect on the imaginative minds of the Brontës.

Anne Brontë deserves to be regarded as a great writer. Our fascination with the Brontës is not going to go away any time soon and, thankfully, interest in Anne is growing. Perhaps paying more attention to what she has to say can teach us empathy and understanding. I like to think she has helped me to make more sense of the people around us and our relationships to each other. Hopefully by the end of this book, you will too.

ONE

THE LIFE AND WORKS OF ANNE

THE EARLY YEARS

The position of perpetual curate of Haworth could not have been offered to Patrick Brontë at a better time. After initially being rejected for the role, he was officially nominated almost a month after the birth of his sixth child, Anne Brontë, in 1820. Anne was the youngest of Patrick and Maria Brontë's children, and the tenth person to make up the household at the parsonage in Thornton, Bradford, where Patrick had been perpetual curate for five years. As well as Patrick, Maria and six children all under the age of six, there were also the sisters Nancy and Sarah Garrs, two servants employed by the family. The position in Haworth presented an opportunity for Patrick to increase his wage, and the parsonage there offered much more space for the young family.[1]

The Brontë children (Maria, Elizabeth, Charlotte, Branwell and Emily) spent the day of Anne's birth at Kipping House, the home of their friends the Firths. John Scholefield Firth was a doctor, and his daughter Elizabeth Firth became Anne's godmother, along with her friend Fanny Outhwaite, and their friendship with and love for the Brontë family continued even after the family moved to Haworth. Anne's Bible was a

Anne's birthplace at Thornton, Bradford.

christening gift from Elizabeth, who inscribed the flyleaf with 'To Anne Brontë with the love & best wishes of her Godmother Elizabeth Firth.' Her father also wrote, 'Remember, my dear Child, frequently to read this Book, with much prayer to God — and to keep it all your life-time, for the sake of the Donor.' The Bible was presented to Anne when it was decided that she was old enough to have it – there is an inscription in pencil at the front of the book, in what looks to be Patrick's handwriting, which reads, 'Keep this till Anne is 10 years of age.'[2]

When Anne was almost three months old, the Brontë family said goodbye to their good friends in Thornton and travelled to Haworth parsonage. The final stretch of their journey, from the bottom of Main Street to the parsonage itself, can still be walked today and many of the buildings are still the same now as they were then. Main Street is very steep and still cobbled, begging the question, 'How on earth did horse-drawn carts make it up and down here?' The Haworth of today is very proud of its literary heritage: the bookshops are full of Brontë editions and related works; the tea rooms are named after Brontë books and characters, and everyone seems to have a story or two about the family. In one day, I learned of two chairs that are both claimed to be Branwell's – the chair in the stairway of the Black Bull Inn was pointed out to me as the *real* one, but earlier I had been told by a volunteer at the museum that the chair was kept in the parsonage itself.

The family barely even had a year to settle into life at Haworth before their mother, Maria Brontë, became dangerously ill with cancer of the uterus. She died on 15 September 1821. Her eldest daughter, Maria, was just eight years old, and Anne was four months from her second birthday. Being so young, it's unlikely that Anne had any of her own memories of their mother.

All of the Brontës carried the loss with them for the rest of their lives, but Anne was to grow up with plenty of affection and loving role models. There was Patrick, their driven, well-educated and loving father. Maria took on the role of mother to her younger sisters and brother, and was a bright, intelligent child (she could read French by age ten[3]). There isn't much left to us of Elizabeth, except that she was loving, dependable and willing to take on household duties.[4] Charlotte, Branwell and Emily all grew to be imaginative, intellectual and intense in their own ways. Their 'darling' Anne, the baby of the family, cannot have failed to be influenced by such a diverse collection of relatives.[5] For their part, the older children were very pleased with their baby sister, making her the pet of the family and watching over her.[6] Charlotte, as a young child, even claimed to have seen an angel standing at Anne's bedside.[7]

Anne's aunt, Elizabeth Branwell, became a permanent member of the household after the death of Maria. She had travelled from her home in Penzance to care for her dying sister, and her stay was only ever meant to be temporary. But knowing that the children would need another parental figure and that Patrick wouldn't be able to look after six children alone on top of his duties as curate, she agreed to stay until the children went to school. In fact, Aunt Branwell spent the rest of her life with the Brontës in Haworth, 'behaving as an affectionate mother to my children,' wrote Patrick.[8] She became an especially big influence on Anne; they shared a room together during Anne's childhood, and Anne spent most of her time with Aunt Branwell when the older children were later away at school.

There were six young children, two adults and two servants living in the parsonage. The 'children's room' (which later became Emily's room) still has faint drawings on the walls, presumed to have been made by the Brontë children. This image of the Brontës scribbling on the walls, acting the part of creative and mischievous children, is at odds with the general perception that they were quiet and subdued, watched over by a stern and distant father and a strict spinster aunt.

Mrs Gaskell describes the young Brontës' room as a room for study, rather than play, and doesn't fail to remind the reader of the tragic lives of the family: 'This little extra up-stairs room was appropriated to the children. Small as it was, it was not called a nursery; indeed, it had not the comfort of a fireplace in it; the servants—two affectionate, warm-hearted sisters, who cannot now speak of the family without tears—called the room the "children's study."'[9] She goes on to say that the children were 'grave and silent beyond their years',[10] and takes many opportunities to describe their father as withdrawn and eccentric. Aunt Branwell receives a particularly harsh description as someone respected by the children, but not loved.[11]

As well as the drawings on the wall of the children's room, there are many anecdotes that contradict Mrs Gaskell's image of a group of sombre children. Some of them are even recorded in Mrs Gaskell's *Life*, and in reading it I have to question why only the tragic, dreary parts of the Brontës' lives have seemed to stick. Mrs Gaskell tried to paint Charlotte as a dutiful daughter and sister, whose life was a struggle; she tried to make Charlotte into the perfect Victorian woman to counter the criticisms she and her sisters received about their writing being distasteful. Charlotte's life was presented as a string of tragedies and sacrifices – mix that with the very human tendency to fixate on the more morbid parts of a story, and it's easier to understand why, even when presented with the contrary, readers preferred the sad version of the Brontë narrative.

In contrast to this, we have an anecdote from Patrick himself about life with his children, from a letter he wrote to Mrs Gaskell:

> When mere children, as soon as they could read and write, Charlotte and her brother and sisters used to invent and act little plays of their own, in which the Duke of Wellington, my daughter Charlotte's hero, was sure to come off conqueror; when a dispute would not unfrequently arise amongst them regarding the comparative merits of him, Buonaparte, Hannibal, and Ceasar. When the argument got warm, and rose to its height, as their mother was then dead, I had sometimes to come in as arbitrator, and settle the dispute according to the best of my judgement. Generally, in the management of these concerns, I frequently thought that I discovered signs of rising talent, which I had seldom or never before seen in any of their age.[12]

Clearly the children were unafraid of incurring their father's wrath, as it sounds like Patrick's intervention was a regular necessity.

Sarah Garrs' recollections also contradict Mrs Gaskell's description of the children. She spent a lot of time with them, walking on the moors and teaching the girls how to sew. 'Their fun knew no bounds,' according to her. 'It occasioned many a merry burst of laughter. They enjoyed a game of romps, and played with zest.'[13]

Their father took a great deal of interest in their education, and the children took their lessons with him until he felt that the older children should attend school. He was well aware of their intelligence, as illustrated by one incident in which he asked questions of his children while they were in disguise. His theory was that the children might feel less self-conscious if they were allowed to speak from behind a mask. When asked what a child like her most wanted, the four-year-old

Anne replied, 'Age and experience'.

Emily, when asked what should be done about her brother Branwell (who was sometimes 'a naughty boy'), replied that her father should 'reason with him, and when he won't listen, whip him'. Charlotte was asked her opinion on the best book in the world and answered, 'The Bible.' Her next best was 'The Book of Nature'.[14]

All their answers speak of acumen beyond their years. Anne's, in particular, was always funny to me, and indicative of the kind of person that she would become. As the youngest in a large family, she would have quickly become familiar with the sibling hierarchy defined by age, and wished for more of those things that would let her climb that ladder.

In 1824, sisters Maria, Elizabeth, Charlotte and Emily were sent to the Clergy Daughters' School at Cowan Bridge, the now infamous school that was exaggerated and immortalised by Charlotte as Lowood School in *Jane Eyre*. This left Branwell (aged seven) and Anne (four) at home with their father, Aunt Branwell and the Garrs sisters.

It was originally Patrick's intention that Anne should follow her sisters to the Clergy Daughters' School, but Anne didn't actually go to school until she was fifteen. On 14 February 1825, Maria was sent home from school with tuberculosis. Patrick and Aunt Branwell did everything they could to nurse her back to health, but she passed away on 6 May. Elizabeth also fell ill and she too was sent home on 31 May. Patrick himself went to collect Charlotte and Emily the very next day, and they never returned to the Clergy Daughters' School. Elizabeth died on 15 June 1825.

Maria and Elizabeth had become surrogate mothers to their younger siblings after the death of their mother, and now they were gone too. They had always been a close family, but after three huge losses in such a short amount of time, their bonds became even tighter. All four children remained at home with their father and aunt for the next six years.

'THE YOUNG MEN'

The next few months saw a routine slowly return to the parsonage. Charlotte and Emily once again joined Branwell and Anne on their walks across the moors and took part in lessons with their father and aunt. A new servant, a local woman named Tabitha (Tabby) Aykroyd, had replaced Sarah and Nancy Garrs (Sarah had left to get married, and Patrick had helped Nancy to find a new position). It wasn't long before the young Brontës were back to their plays – and began playfully terrorising Tabby. Francis Leyland, a friend of Branwell's, recorded an instance of the plays becoming too much for her: 'On one occasion, with increased energy of action and voice, they so wrought on her fears that she retreated to her nephew's house', exclaiming that the children had 'all goon mad'.[15]

Their plays began to take on a deeper significance in 1826 when Branwell received a set of toy soldiers from Patrick, who had brought them back from a trip to Leeds. Charlotte recorded the event in her diary in 1829:

> Papa bought Branwell some soldiers at Leeds. When Papa came home it was night and we where in Bed so next morning Branwell came to our Door with a Box of soldiers. Emily and I jumped out of Bed and I snat[c] hed up one and exclaimed this the Duke of Wellington it shall be mine!! When I said this Emily likewise took one and said it should be hers. When Anne came down she took one also. Mine was the prettiest of the whole and perfect in every part. Emilys was a Grave looking fellow

> [and] we called him Gravey. Anne's was a queer little thing very much like herself [and] he was called Waiting Boy. Branwell chose Bonaparte.[16]

Anne's oddly named Waiting Boy eventually became Sir James Clark Ross, ruler of Rossessland in a fictional part of Africa called Glass Town. He was named after the historical figure of the same name, an explorer who had accompanied the Arctic explorer Sir William Edward Parry. Parry became the namesake of Emily's soldier Gravey, whose land was named Parrysland. Charlotte's soldier ruled over Wellingtonsland, and Branwell's Bonaparte took on many different aliases, including Sneaky of Sneakysland.

They had made other plays before, and continued to make new ones afterwards, but none had the impact or the endurance of 'The Young Men'. As their plays grew in scale, the children began to write them down, inventing whole stories for each character. Branwell even wrote himself and his sisters into their imagined world, naming himself Brannii, one of the Chief Gennii. Charlotte, Emily and Anne became Tallii, Emmii and Annii, each the protector of their chosen soldier. They made tiny books out of scraps of paper, in which they wrote their 'Histories', newspapers, epic poetry, maps and everything else related to the plays and the stories they made up around them.

The events that took place in the plays were inspired by their voracious reading (see Chapter Seven), and the children would act out their plays and then record them quickly and energetically in their miniature books in both prose and poetry. There was also a competitive nature to them – if a man was taken prisoner or killed, it wouldn't take long for that man's protective Genii to compose a scathing retaliation in which the offending Genii was ridiculed, the opposing men exposed as fools, and the prisoners released and brought back to life. They spurred each other on to create sprawling, epic tales of romance, revenge and betrayal. Between them they created something comparable to a naïve version of *Game of Thrones*.

This scribblemania continued throughout their teenage years, the Glass Town saga eventually becoming Angria, a place as violent and dangerous as the name suggests. When Charlotte went to Roe Head School in 1831, it gave Emily and Anne the chance to break away from the super-masculine plays of Angria and the influence of Charlotte and Branwell. They took some of their Glass Town characters and created a new play better suited to their own tastes. The result was Gondal and Gaaldine, lands that reflected their love of the Yorkshire moors and what they had read of the Scottish Highlands, and which featured a host of powerful female characters.

The only Gondal-related works that have survived are the Gondal poems, lists of place names and characters made by Anne,[17] and Anne and Emily's 'Diary Papers', which were written every four years, beginning on 24 November 1834. Gondal continued to be a collaborative venture for the rest of their lives, though it appears that Anne became much less invested in Gondal over time.

Charlotte's friend Ellen Nussey remarked in her *Reminiscences* that Anne and Emily were 'like twins—inseparable companions, and in the very closest sympathy, which never had any interruption'.[18] The idea of Emily and Anne as close companions has remained solid since the very earliest biographies of the Brontës. Even in her groundbreaking biography of Anne published in 1959, Winifred Gérin wrote that Anne's Gondal poems about separation from a loved one and imprisonment were about how she felt when she and Emily were separated by school and, later, their employment.[19] While they were close Gondal collaborators in childhood, and Anne was even persuaded to play at Gondal while on a trip to York with Emily as adults, Anne and Emily's tastes gradually grew apart.

ANNE AT SCHOOL

Anne and Emily's first separation since developing Gondal came when first Emily and then Anne went to Roe Head School, run by Miss Wooler. Charlotte had attended Roe Head in 1831 and she was invited back in July 1835 as a teacher. As part of her payment, one of her sisters was invited to the school as a pupil for free. Emily, as the eldest, was the first to join Charlotte at the school. But homesickness proved to be too much for her, and she returned home in October. Anne replaced her at the school – at the age of fifteen, she was to receive her first formal education.

It is reasonable to think that Anne suffered from homesickness, just as Emily did. This was her first time away from home, and while Miss Wooler's school was a far cry from the terrible conditions at Cowan Bridge, it was still a big change for Anne. There were new routines to get used to, and her days would be much more structured than they were at home. There was no more opportunity for wandering out onto the moors.

Roe Head School, drawn by Anne.

Anne and Charlotte appear to have been estranged while at school, as Charlotte kept her distance. Her authority as a teacher may have been one reason for that, but she was also experiencing a personal crisis at the time; she knew she needed to earn a living but she resented being surrounded by and having to teach girls she referred to as 'fatheaded oafs'.[20]

If Anne was miserable at school, she didn't make it obvious to anyone. She was likely aware of the opportunity she had been given, and which she may never have had if Emily hadn't left. She also knew that she would need to gain employment some day, and as her most likely future employment would be as a governess, she needed the correct training for such a role. Anne performed her duty as a diligent student, earning a prize from the school at the end of her first year, a copy of Watt's *On The Improvement of the Mind* with an inscription by Miss Wooler: 'Prize for good conduct presented to Miss A. Brontë with Miss Wooler's kind love, Roe Head, Dec. 14th 1836.'[21]

Conducting her duties didn't stop Anne from writing, as it never would when she was older, and her three earliest extant poems were written while she was a student. 'Verses by Lady Geralda', 'Alexander and Zenobia' and 'A Voice from the Dungeon' were all Gondal poems, and all dealt with loss of different kinds, from the parting of lovers, to the melancholy longing of a prisoner who knows they are to 'live and die alone'.[22] There is the temptation here to view Anne's poems as representative of her experience at Roe Head; that they were essentially autobiographical verses but Anne disguised herself as Gondal characters, pining for home and happier times. However, Barker notes that even though she was at home, Emily's Gondal poetry from the same time follows similar themes, which were fairly common within the Gondal poems in general.[23]

In late 1837, Anne suddenly became very ill. The cause of her illness has been attributed to different things by different biographers, including Mrs Gaskell's account that Anne suffered only from a common cold, and Charlotte, 'stung by anxiety for this little sister', exaggerated Anne's symptoms.[24] What Mrs Gaskell does not mention is that a Moravian minister, Reverend James La Trobe, visited Anne several times during her illness and stated that 'She was suffering from a severe attack of gastric fever which brought her very low, and her voice was only a whisper; her life hung on a slender thread.'[25]

The presence of a Moravian minister leads to discussions about the religious crisis Anne experienced (see Chapter Five) and which no doubt aggravated her illness. She left Roe Head School in December 1837, returning to the parsonage in Haworth.

A WORKING LIFE

By 1839, all four of the Brontës were back at home. Charlotte had left Miss Wooler's school, Branwell had left his studio in Bradford (where he had tried to earn his living as a portrait painter), and Emily had left her short-lived job as a teacher at Law Hill school in Halifax. Anne was just nineteen, and homesickness and loneliness had accompanied her time spent at Roe Head, but this didn't stop her from attempting to find employment as a governess. Anne displayed a tenacity and willingness to push herself into new experiences in a way that wasn't necessarily expected of the baby of the family. She found work at Blake Hall in Mirfield, where she was to be governess to the two eldest children of Mr and Mrs Joshua Ingham – Cunliffe, aged six, and Mary, his five-year-old sister.[26]

The stately stone mansion that was Blake Hall, and its finely kept gardens, reflected the wealth of the Ingham family. This was Anne's first introduction to the lives and habits of wealthy people, an important experience that found its way into both of Anne's novels. Joshua Ingham was a local squire, magistrate and businessman, and he was somewhat of a tyrant. Edward Chitham writes that 'one of Ingham's daughters told how she was looking in a mirror at her ringlets one day. Her father, catching sight of her through an open door, cut off all her hair to punish her vanity.'[27]

If Anne kept a diary it no longer survives, and there is no Diary Paper that was written in the year that Anne was at Blake Hall. Neither do we have any letters that Anne wrote during her time there, though we know that she wrote at least one to her family back home. Charlotte refers to this letter in her correspondence with Ellen Nussey: she relates that Anne's charges are 'desperate little dunces' that Anne has to 'scold, coax and threaten' as she is 'not empowered to inflict any punishment'. Charlotte describes Anne as a 'poor child' who was so quiet that her new employer might assume she had a speech impediment, and she also tells Ellen that she would be 'astonished to see what a sensible, clever letter she writes'.[28] There's a mix of pride and of concern – of surprise at the youngest sister's abilities while also implying that she hardly expected Anne to be capable of writing such a letter.

While it's easy to read Charlotte's portrayal of Anne as patronising and even passive aggressive, Charlotte is staunchly on her sister's side when it comes to the behaviour of the children, and Anne's plight as teacher. She never questions Anne's descriptions of their behaviour nor does she criticise Anne's methods of dealing with them, at least not to Ellen. Having been a teacher herself, it's likely that Charlotte could empathise with the struggles that Anne was now facing.

The only other anecdotes available to us regarding Anne's

time at Blake Hall come from Susan Brooke, whose grandmother was a sister of one of Anne's pupils. Two of those stories concern the terrible behaviour of the children. In one instance, the children received a gift of some bright red South American cloaks. They immediately put them on and ran out into the park, shouting and screaming and calling themselves devils. Anne tried to coax them back inside, but eventually broke down and was forced to retrieve Mrs Ingham. The second story goes that, after a particularly long day of unpleasant behaviour on behalf of the children, Anne tied them to a table leg so that she could get on with some writing.[29]

Both these stories deal with Anne's struggle to discipline the children; they knew that their governess was not allowed to issue punishment, and that she had to go to their mother with behavioural complaints. Going to their mother too often would have given the idea that Anne had no control over the children, which had effectively already been taken away from her by their mother in the first place. It was certainly a difficult situation for Anne to find herself in, and she was eventually dismissed in December 1839, with the Inghams citing Anne's failure to produce any improvement in their children as the cause.[30]

Anne returned home to find a new face frequenting the parsonage. William Weightman was Patrick's new curate, and much has been said about Anne's romantic interest in him. Charlotte certainly seemed to think that something was going on, and wrote to Ellen of a morning spent in church: 'He sits opposite Anne at church sighing softly and looking out of the corners of his eyes to win her attention – and Anne is so quiet, her look so down-cast, they are a picture.'[31]

Weightman quickly became a favourite in the parsonage – and with Ellen Nussey too. He sent all four girls a Valentine in February 1840 and, to avoid detection, he walked ten miles to Bradford to post them. The Brontës and Ellen quickly discovered that he was the one responsible and sent him a short poem back, expressing their gratitude and their delight.[32]

Though Winifred Gérin and others have said that Anne was in love with Weightman, Juliet Barker argues that it was actually Charlotte who fell for the young, and by all accounts handsome, curate. Her letters to Ellen were full of accounts of Weightman, and even after it became apparent that he wasn't interested in her romantically, she wrote often of what she determined to be his flirtatious manner, and of how he and Anne were pining for each other. She gave him the nickname Celia Amelia, referring to his often feminine ways and charm.[33] But his time at Haworth was tragically cut short when he fell ill with cholera. He died on 6 September 1842 and was buried in Haworth church by Patrick himself. Patrick was visibly distressed when he delivered the funeral sermon, declaring that he and Weightman were 'always like father and son'.[34]

Whatever her feelings for Weightman may have been, Anne didn't allow herself a long holiday after leaving Blake Hall. By May 1840, she was back in employment again, this time as

Charlotte's portrait of William Weightman.

governess to the five children of Mr and Mrs Robinson, who were the wealthy inhabitants of Thorp Green Hall. Once again, Anne's tenacity and determination to be useful overpowered any sense of defeat she must have felt at losing her last job. Thorp Green was a grand hall located between York, Ripon and Harrogate, which back then was populated mostly by wealthy farmers on rich agricultural land. The house itself was more than twice the size of Blake Hall, with huge areas of surrounding parkland.

For the next five years, until June 1845, Anne spent almost all her time with the Robinson family. There were short breaks at Christmas and in the summer, during which she was free to visit her family, but these were only for two or three weeks at a time. It was during this period that Anne started to drift further away from Gondal and the sweeping epic poems set in the fantasy worlds she had created with her brother and sisters, and started to employ more sophisticated realism in her writing. Gondal poems were generally written while Anne was back home with Emily, and during her early days at Thorp Green her poems started to reflect some of the homesickness and self-doubt that she was feeling.[35]

Anne was responsible for the four eldest children, including Edmund, the only boy, whom she also had to tutor. Anne had a peculiar advantage over other prospective governesses in this respect, as she had received something of a classical education, thanks to her father. He had taught Branwell and, in a move that would have been considered very progressive, had allowed his daughters to learn alongside their brother. Anne even bought a Latin textbook in 1843, presumably to aid in teaching Edmund.[36]

The Robinsons, while maybe not Anne's preferred company, nevertheless offered her opportunities that she would have been unlikely to experience without their influence. She went on trips to York with the family, where she admired the deeply historical city and York Minster. The Robinsons also spent their summers in Scarborough, which is where Anne had her first glimpse of the sea. There's no doubt that it became one of Anne's favourite places, and her love of the sea often made its way into her work (see Chapter Four).

A Diary Paper by Anne from July 1841 tells us about her first year with the Robinsons as governess, and what she hoped for herself over the next four years. It reveals her capacity for self-criticism and a constant desire to better herself. She acknowledges that she still has the 'same faults' as she did when she was at school, but suggests that she is better equipped now to deal with them – she has some of the experience that she wished for when her father had asked her what a child like her most wanted. Her self-deprecation is evident in the final lines, in which she dismisses her own thoughts – that the age of twenty-five would be important to her – as 'a superstitious fantasy'.[37]

In this Diary Paper Anne also states that she dislikes her job and wishes for another: 'We are thinking of setting up a school of our own but nothing definite is settled about it yet.' The idea of a school had been floating around between the Brontës for a while – running their own school would give them the freedom that being a governess or a teacher in someone else's school would not, and Charlotte had even asked Miss Wooler for her advice. But school plans were delayed when Charlotte and Emily left Haworth in February 1842 to attend the Pensionnat Héger in Brussels, in order to improve their French and German and therefore make their potential future school more attractive. Anne was left behind.

In October that year, their Aunt Branwell died. The Brontës made their way home, but only Anne and Branwell were there in time for the funeral. The Robinsons allowed Anne to spend a few weeks with her family, where she was briefly reunited with Emily and Charlotte, before she returned to Thorp Green. Emily stayed in Haworth, but Charlotte returned to Brussels as a teacher, further delaying the school plans.

By the time that Anne wrote her next Diary Paper in 1845, she had just left Thorp Green, the school plans had come to nothing, and all the Brontës were unemployed and at home again. She writes about the world of Gondal, but wonders how it will fare in the future, given that 'The Gondals in general are not in first rate playing condition—will they improve?'[38]

By contrast, Emily's Diary Paper written at the same time makes much of the fact that she and Anne had played Gondal on their visit to York in June: 'The Gondals still flo[u]rish bright as ever [...] We intend sticking by the rascals as long as they delight us which I am glad to say they do at present.'[39] A comparison of the two makes it clear that Anne was much less willing to spend her time thinking and writing about Gondal, but Emily was apparently oblivious to this, which suggests that Anne may have been keeping her interest in Gondal alive in part for Emily's benefit.

The lodgings in Scarborough, where Anne spent summers with the Robinsons.

To an outsider they may still have appeared to be as close as twins, but Anne's mood at that time could not have been more different to Emily's. Her Diary Paper at that time gives some more context around Anne's concerns in relation to her experiences at Thorp Green: she writes about having only just 'escaped' and how wretched she would have been four years earlier if she knew she would still be at Thorp Green in 1845. She also writes about the 'very unpleasant and undreamt of experiences of human nature' she witnessed while working for the Robinsons. These experiences have long been a source of interest and speculation for anyone interested in the Brontës.[40]

In 1843, Branwell had accompanied Anne back to Thorp Green, to start a new job as tutor to Edmund Robinson. It is now generally accepted that Branwell had an affair with Mrs Robinson, which resulted in his dismissal not long after Anne had resigned her post. He never recovered from the end of his liaison and was convinced that Mrs Robinson would be free and willing to marry him after her husband's death. But in 1847 she relocated to Birmingham and married Sir Edward Scott. The Brontës saw this as behaviour typical of such a woman: she laid the blame for the affair at Branwell's feet, refused any communication with him, and secured herself a wealthy husband. Three years after the trouble started, the after-effects were still being felt and Charlotte wrote to Ellen Nussey of her deep dislike for Mrs Robinson.[41]

But the reason for Anne's resignation and her subsequent melancholy cannot all be blamed on Branwell and his misconduct. Lydia, Elizabeth and Mary, the three oldest Robinson girls, were close to reaching the stage at which they no longer needed a governess. Lydia even caused a scandal of her own when she eloped, aged just eighteen. The two younger girls were at the mercy of their mother, who arranged engagements for the both of them. Their age, plus the behaviour of their mother, had possibly cemented Anne's decision to leave even before she knew that Branwell was having an affair with Mrs Robinson.

It would be unfair to assume that Anne's time at Thorp Green was completely miserable, however. Elizabeth and Mary Robinson clearly held a lot of affection for Anne and continued to correspond with her even after she left. They also gave her a dog, named Flossy, who became the subject of a few sketches and paintings made by Anne and Emily. The two Robinson girls even visited Anne in Haworth long after she left Thorp Green.[42]

In 1845, the Brontës were once again all at home and Branwell continued to decline. He fell into drinking and gambling, and even began to make a habit of taking opium. By 1848, Branwell's condition had worsened to the point that Charlotte wrote to Ellen, 'Branwell is the same in conduct as ever – his constitution seems much shattered – Papa – and sometimes all of us have sad nights with him – he sleeps most of the day, and consequently will lie awake at night – But has not every house its trial?'[43]

It was against this backdrop of despair that Anne, Charlotte and Emily began to seriously consider their literary careers. Anne may have been looking for more governess positions, but whatever her plans might have been at that time, their lives were suddenly taken over once again by the scribblemania of their youth. Charlotte discovered Emily's poems in the late autumn of 1845, and their first book of collected poems, simply titled *Poems, by Currer, Ellis and Acton Bell*, was published in 1846.

Charlotte's infamous 'Biographical Notice of Ellis and Acton Bell', which featured in the 1850 edition of *Wuthering Heights* and *Agnes Grey*, gives us the story of how Charlotte 'accidentally lighted on' Emily's poetry, which she describes as 'condensed and terse, vigorous and genuine. To my ear, they had also a peculiar music – wild, melancholy, and elevating.' About Anne's efforts she writes:

> Meantime, my younger sister quietly produced some of her own compositions, intimating that since Emily's had given me pleasure, I might like to look at hers. I could not but be a partial judge, yet I thought that these verses too had a sweet sincere pathos of their own.[44]

Ignoring for a moment what could be read as a dismissal of Anne's poetry as inferior, Charlotte's assertion that she discovered Emily's poetry by accident is sugar-coating it in the extreme. We know from Emily's Diary Papers that she kept her manuscripts in a small tin, away from prying eyes, and didn't even share what she was writing with Anne ('she is writing some poetry too[.] I wonder what it is about.')[45] Emily must have been furious (and Charlotte makes it clear that she had to work hard to persuade Emily to publish the poems), but Anne's offering of her own poetry may have been an attempt to calm the situation. If Emily was going to have her own private work thrown out into the open, then so should she.

While preparing their poems for publication, the sisters were also working on their novels: Charlotte on *The Professor*, Emily on *Wuthering Heights*, and Anne on *Agnes Grey*. Once they had been completed, the sisters sent them to as many publishers as they could find. *Wuthering Heights* and *Agnes Grey* found a publisher in Thomas Cautley Newby and were published together in December 1847. Remarkably, Anne's second novel, *The Tenant of Wildfell Hall*, was published just six months later, in June 1848.

'A DREADFUL DARKNESS CLOSES IN'

1848 saw more family tragedy arrive at the parsonage. Branwell's health had continued to worsen. The early symptoms of tuberculosis may have been masked by the effects of alcohol and opium abuse, but the seriousness of his illness was soon realised. Branwell died on 24 September 1848, aged thirty-one, his last words to his friend John Brown being an expression of his regrets: 'In all my past life I have done nothing either great or good.'[46]

At Branwell's funeral, Emily began to display the signs of a common cold. After a brief, tense illness, made all the more unbearable for her family by her refusal to see a doctor, Emily too succumbed to tuberculosis. She died on 19 December, aged just thirty.

Anne, Charlotte and Patrick spent the winter grieving and dealing with the colds, flus and coughs that they always suffered from around this time of year. Though it's often portrayed that Anne was the weakest Brontë in terms of health, and had always been frail, the whole household had always been susceptible to bad colds in the winter.

Anne's terrible cough, which sometimes developed alongside colds and flus, was the result of asthma. She had been troubled by it since birth, and it has always been a source of contention for me that her asthma should see her portrayed as weak and delicate. In the days before prescription inhalers, Anne would have had to sit out every attack of asthma and wait for it to pass. She would have to remain calm and quiet – two other words that are often associated with her but which usually take on negative connotations. For Anne, in the midst of an asthma attack, to keep calm would have been paramount to keeping herself alive. It undoubtedly had a hand in shaping her personality; she could work well under terrible conditions, she kept a lot of complaints to herself, and she often appeared as the calm, logical peacekeeper.

Anne's bout of illness over the winter after Emily's death was no different. She suffered more than Charlotte and developed a cough that would not go away. But when she started to complain of a pain in her side, a sign of tuberculosis, a doctor was immediately called for. He confirmed the diagnosis, which was effectively a death sentence at the time.

Unlike Emily, Anne did everything she could to prolong her own life. She accepted every treatment that was recommended. Mrs Gaskell wrote: 'All through this illness of Anne's, Charlotte had the comfort of being able to talk to her about her state; a comfort rendered inexpressibly great by the contrast which it presented to the recollection of Emily's rejection of all sympathy. If a proposal for Anne's benefit was made, Charlotte could speak to her about it, and the nursing and the dying sister could consult with each other as to its desirability.'[47]

Anne's desire to try any kind of cure prompted her to suggest a change of surroundings. She wished to visit York and Scarborough again, and tried to persuade Charlotte that they should go, but she was very reluctant to let Anne travel. In her desperation to try a seaside cure, Anne wrote to Ellen Nussey, almost pleading with her to accompany them to Scarborough and to help her convince Charlotte of the plan. This last letter by Anne, written in April 1849, goes against everything that is said of her willingness to join God, of her passive acceptance of death. Only if her chances of survival were nought could she maybe accept death, but until then she was going to do everything in her power to make sure that her 'humble schemes' should come to fruition.[48]

Anne eventually persuaded Charlotte to accompany her to Scarborough. Fanny Outhwaite, in her final act of kindness towards her god-daughter, had left £200 to Anne in her will. Fanny, of course, would have hoped that the money should be used for something happier, but as it was, this inheritance ensured Anne's comfort on what was to be her final trip. They set out for Scarborough, stopping in York for an evening so that they could purchase new clothes and visit York Minster, a cathedral that she loved. Ellen wrote that the visit to the Minster was an 'overpowering pleasure' for Anne, who was very happy to be back in York.[49]

In Scarborough, Anne tried to do as many of the things that she enjoyed as possible. She went to the bath house, drove across the beach in a cart pulled by a donkey, and went to church on the Sunday morning.[50] She tried to carry out what she had said to Ellen in her letter – she had not come to Scarborough to die, but for a change of scenery. Charlotte and Ellen were not her nurses, but her companions.

Anne passed away in their lodgings in Scarborough, overlooking the sea, on 28 May 1849. Her last words, on seeing Charlotte's grief, were 'Take courage Charlotte! Take Courage.'[51] Anne was the only Brontë not to be buried in the church in Haworth. Her grave is in Scarborough, in the cliff-top churchyard of St Mary's. In her final letter to Ellen, Anne had expressed a wish to 'do some good in this world'. If she could see how *The Tenant of Wildfell Hall* has sparked debate on gender equality, the education of girls, and the rights of women within marriage, she might be proud.

Helen sketches the view over the beach as Gilbert watches, in an illustration by Walter L. Colls from a 1901 edition of The Tenant of Wildfell Hall.

CHRONOLOGY OF ANNE'S LIFE & WORKS

1820 Anne Brontë is born on 17 January at Thornfield. She is the youngest child of the Reverend Patrick Brontë and Maria Branwell. She has four older sisters and one brother. In April of this year, the family moves to Haworth, where Patrick Brontë was perpetual curate.

1821 Anne's mother Maria dies from cancer on 15 September. Elizabeth Branwell, who had originally come to care for her sister, remains at Haworth to help look after the Brontë children.

1824 Anne's two eldest sisters, Maria and Elizabeth, attend the Clergy Daughters' School at Cowan Bridge from July. Charlotte follows in August, Emily follows in November. Four-year-old Anne remains at home.

1825 Maria returns home from Cowan Bridge with tuberculosis on 14 February and dies on 6 May. Elizabeth is sent home ill on 31 May, and Charlotte and Emily leave for home the next day. Elizabeth dies on 15 June.

1826 Branwell receives a gift of toy soldiers from his father. These soldiers become the inspiration for siblings' imaginary worlds: the Glass Town Confederacy, Angria and Gondal. The children remain together in Haworth until 1830, under the care of their Aunt Branwell.

1829 The Brontë children receive art lessons from John Bradley of Keighley.

1831 Charlotte attends Margaret Wooler's school at Roe Head. While there, she meets Mary Taylor and Ellen Nussey, who become lifelong friends.

1832 Charlotte leaves Roe Head in June.

1834 Anne and Emily write their first Diary Paper. It includes the earliest existing reference to Gondal.

1835 Charlotte returns to Roe Head as a teacher in July. Emily joins her as a pupil but leaves in October, and Anne takes her place. At fifteen, this is the first time Anne has received formal education.

1837 Anne suffers a serious illness that coincides with a religious crisis. She meets with a Moravian minister, James La Trobe. She leaves Roe Head School in December.

1839 In April, Anne takes up her first employed position, as a governess to the children of Joshua Ingham at Blake Hall, Mirfield. She is dismissed in December.

1840 Anne takes up her second and final post, as governess to the children of Rev. Edmund Robinson at Thorp Green Hall, Little Ouseburn.

1841 Charlotte, Emily and Anne plan to start their own school. Aunt Branwell provides financial help for Charlotte and Emily to attend a school in Brussels, where they can improve their language skills.

1842 Charlotte and Emily enrol at the Pensionnat Héger, Brussels, in February. They return home in November, after the sudden death of their Aunt Branwell on 29 October.

1843 Charlotte returns to Brussels alone. Branwell accompanies Anne back to Thorp Green, where he begins his new job as tutor to the Robinsons' son.

1845 Anne resigns her post at Thorp Green and returns to the parsonage in June. Branwell also returns, after being dismissed as Edmund's tutor after an alleged affair with his employer's wife. Anne and Emily travel to York in June and return in July. In September, Charlotte discovers

Emily's poetry. The sisters arrange a collection of their poetry in the hopes of publication.

1846 *Poems by Currer, Ellis and Acton Bell* is published.

1847 Charlotte's *Jane Eyre* is published in October, by Smith, Elder & Co. In December, Anne's *Agnes Grey* is published by Thomas Cautley Newby alongside Emily's *Wuthering Heights*.

1848 Anne's second novel, *The Tenant of Wildfell Hall*, is published in June. A second edition comes out in August, with a new preface written by Anne. Charlotte and Anne travel to London to visit Charlotte's publisher and prove that they are two separate authors. Branwell dies on 24 September, aged thirty-one. Emily dies on 19 December, aged thirty.

1849 Anne is diagnosed with tuberculosis in January. She travels to Scarborough with Charlotte and Ellen Nussey in May, hoping that it will improve her health. Anne dies on 28 May, aged twenty-nine. She is buried in St Mary's churchyard in Scarborough. Charlotte's second novel, *Shirley*, is published in October.

1850 Charlotte edits *Wuthering Heights* and *Agnes Grey* for republication by Smith, Elder & Co. It is published with a 'Biographical Notice' of Ellis and Acton Bell and a new preface to *Wuthering Heights*, both written by Charlotte. Charlotte also edited a collection of poems by Anne and Emily that were included in this edition.

1853 Charlotte's third novel, *Villette*, is published.

1854 The heavily edited *Parlour Library* edition of *The Tenant of Wildfell Hall* is published by Thomas Hodgson. Charlotte marries Arthur Bell Nicholls, her father's curate, and they honeymoon in Ireland.

1855 Charlotte Brontë dies on 31 March 1855, aged thirty-eight.

1857 Elizabeth Gaskell's *The Life of Charlotte Brontë* is published.

1861 Patrick Brontë dies on 7 June, aged eighty-five.

TWO

ACTON BELL

A WRITING LIFE, OR A LIFE IN WRITING?

Writing was an essential part of life for Anne. It had been a way of entertaining herself and her siblings when she was younger, and this remained partially true as she entered adulthood. But writing started to take on other functions as she matured as both a person and as a writer – she began to write more personal poems, and her prose started to focus more on realism and the daily observations she made of people and experiences.

Very few of Anne's original manuscripts now exist; there are no manuscripts for *Agnes Grey* or *The Tenant of Wildfell Hall*, only five of Anne's letters have been preserved (though it is thought that she wrote hundreds during her lifetime)[1], only four Diary Papers were written by Anne (and two of those were co-written with Emily), and her surviving poetry manuscripts are scattered around private collections and libraries in the UK and the US. While Charlotte and Branwell left behind thousands of words of Glasstown and Angria prose and poetry, none of Emily or Anne's Gondal prose (assuming they wrote any) now exists.

The lack of diary entries by Anne, and the small number of her surviving letters, has fed the trend of reading Brontë material as autobiographical. Winifred Gérin in particular did this extensively in *Anne Brontë: A Biography*, while Edward Chitham wrote in *A Life of Anne Brontë* about the dangers and pitfalls of viewing an author's work as wholly autobiographical. To what extent can we treat Anne's works as autobiographical? When is it appropriate? And why did Anne refer to some of her poems as 'pillars of witness'?[2]

GONDAL

When Anne's poems and two novels were first published in her late twenties, she used the pseudonym Acton Bell. But Anne's writing life began long before 'he' existed. Like many children, the young Brontës created fictional worlds. What made the Brontës unusual was how much they wrote about them, and how their imaginary worlds continued to be a source of creativity well into their adult lives.

In their juvenilia, they mimicked the material they were reading as children and which they admired (see Chapter Seven). Their spelling and grammar were terrible, as if they had tried to get the words onto the pages as quickly as possible. By comparison, their letters seem almost to be written by different people. For example, Anne's Diary Papers are missing a lot of punctuation, and sentences often run into each other. But if you read her letters to Ellen Nussey, they are clear and concise, and generally well put together. It's almost like the difference between how we would write notes to ourselves on our phones, or send texts to those we are close to, and the emails we might send to colleagues or potential employers. We know the rules of language and when to use them, just as the Brontës did.

As we saw in Chapter One, Gondal was the fictional world created by Anne and Emily, and it spawned from the Glass Town and Angria sagas dominated by Charlotte and Branwell. Gondal reflected the different tastes of Anne and Emily compared with those of their brother and older sister. The landscape of Gondal bore many resemblances to the northern landscape of their home, while Angria took place in a much warmer climate, based on what the children read of Africa. Cold stone castles in which heroines and heroes lamented their imprisonment dominate the Gondal saga. The rival families of the four kingdoms of Gondal lent themselves to *Romeo and Juliet*-style romances. The most distinguishing feature of Gondal is its strong-willed heroines, such as Anne's Lady Geralda, who were the driving forces of the action and the plot.

Anne's earliest surviving poem is a Gondal poem. It was written when Anne was sixteen and a pupil at Roe Head. In 'Verses By Lady Geralda' Anne writes on the typical Gondal themes of estrangement and loneliness:

> Why, when I hear the stormy breath
> Of the wild winter wind
> Rushing o'er the mountain heath,
> Does sadness fill my mind?
>
> For long ago I loved to lie
> Upon the pathless moor,
> To hear the wild wind rushing by
> With never ceasing roar;
>
> Its sound was music then to me;
> Its wild and lofty voice
> Made my heart beat exultingly
> And my whole soul rejoice.
>
> But now, how different is the sound?
> It takes another tone,
> And howls along the barren ground
> With melancholy moan […]
>
> O why are things so changed to me?
> What gave me joy before
> Now fills my heart with misery,
> And nature smiles no more.

And why are all the beauties gone
From this my native hill?
Alas! my heart is changed alone:
Nature is constant still.

For when the heart is free from care,
Whatever meets the eye
Is bright, and every sound we hear
Is full of melody [...]

Father! thou hast long been dead,
Mother! thou art gone,
Brother! thou art far away
And I am left alone [...]

But the world's before me now,
Why should I despair?
I will not spend my days in vain,
I will not linger here!

There is still a cherished hope
To cheer me on my way;
It is burning in my heart
With a feeble ray [...]

I leave thee then, my childhood's home,
For all thy joys are gone;
I leave thee through the world to roam
In search of fair renown,

From such a hopeless home to part
Is happiness to me,

For nought can charm my weary ear
Except activity.[3]

The poem was written in December 1836, when Anne was reunited with Emily over the Christmas holidays and they could continue their literary collaboration. It follows an orphan, who finds that the landscape and the scenery of her old home no longer bring her the comforts that they once did, and so she decides to leave that 'hopeless home' to make her own way in the world. The first few verses are indicative of the similarities between the geography of Gondal and that of the moors that Anne preferred to set her imaginary worlds in.

It's tempting to read this as an autobiographical poem, as Anne was homesick while she was away at school and certainly missed her home and her family. Winifred Gérin quoted the poem in her biography and used it as evidence that Anne was feeling depressed at being separated from Emily. Gérin assumed that most of Anne's poems were autobiographical and, in writing about some of Anne's Gondal poems, she suggested that 'Dramatised as the situations are to fit in with the general scheme of Gondal, the feeling is personal and very real.'[4] However, there is plenty of evidence to suggest that it is purely a Gondal poem: it was written when Anne was back at home, it fits with typical dramatic Gondal themes of abandonment and desolation, and, most significantly, it is written from the point of view of a Gondal character, Lady Geralda. Anne is the author of the poem, but the narrator is someone very different.

Anne wrote two more Gondal poems while she was a pupil at Roe Head: 'Alexander and Zenobia' (1 July 1837) and 'A Voice From The Dungeon' (October 1837). The first of these two was presumably written over the summer, when once again Anne was reunited with Emily. The poem is a romantic telling of two Gondal lovers journeying to meet each other after a long separation, a theme that is repeated in some of her later Gondal poems. 'A Voice From The Dungeon' is signed 'Marina Sabia' – her husband and her son are gone (it isn't made clear where to) and she lives alone. Her home has become a dungeon without the presence of her departed family:

I'm buried now; I've done with life;
I've done with hate, revenge and strife;
I've done with joy, with hope and love
And all the bustling world above.

Long have I dwelt forgotten here
In pining woe and dull despair;
This place of solitude and gloom
Must be my dungeon and my tomb [...]

Just then I heard in whisper sweet
A well known voice my name repeat.
His father stood before my eyes;
I gazed at him in mute surprise,

I thought he smiled and spoke to me,
But still in silent ecstasy
I gazed at him; I could not speak;
I uttered one long piercing shriek.

Alas! Alas! That cursed scream
Aroused me from my heavenly dream;
I looked around in wild despair,
I called them, but they were not there;

The father and the child are gone,
And I must live and die alone.[5]

It was not long after writing this that Anne became ill while at school. Her illness was physical but she was also at that time undergoing a religious crisis (see Chapter Five). With this hindsight it is easy to read into this poem echoes of Anne's feeling at the time, especially in the descriptions of loneliness in the first few passages. But it is difficult to say for sure whether external events in Anne's life have any direct parallels in her Gondal poetry.

The worlds of Glass Town and Gondal were playgrounds in which Anne could exert her imagination in any way she liked, unrestricted by real life. Both Anne and Emily may have been inspired by the real cultural and political events that were happening at the time (Emily, for example, was fascinated by the young Princess Victoria and her life, and Mary, Queen of Scots was a source of fascination to all of the Brontës)[6], but we don't know enough about the daily lives of Anne and Emily to be able to say for definite that they were represented in the Gondal poems.

'PILLARS OF WITNESS'

The line between fantasy and reality was often blurred in Emily's case and it's difficult to distinguish between her Gondal and non-Gondal poetry. This difficulty does not present itself when looking at Anne's poetry, and there is a definite distinction between her Gondal poems and those that took on a more realistic tone. As she got older, Anne began to move away from the sweeping, dramatic style of her Gondal poetry, towards a simpler approach. Her poetry became more intimate, more introspective, as she began to write on themes and ideas that were important to her.

The more personal of Anne's poems have come to be referred to as 'pillars of witness', based on a quote from *Agnes Grey* in which Agnes talks about the power of poetry to provide comfort and sympathy:

> When we are harassed by sorrows or anxieties, or long oppressed by any powerful feelings which we must keep to ourselves, for which we can obtain and seek no sympathy from any living creature, and which, yet, we cannot, or will not wholly crush, we often, naturally, seek relief in poetry – and often find it too – whether in the effusions of others, which seem to harmonise with our existing case, or in our own attempts to give utterance to those thoughts and feelings and strains less musical, perchance, but more appropriate, and therefore more penetrating and sympathetic [...]
>
> [...] when suffering from home-sick melancholy, I had sought relief twice or thrice at this secret source of consolation; and now I flew to it again, with greater avidity than ever, because I seemed to need it more. I still preserve those relics of past sufferings and experience, like pillars of witness set up in travelling through the vale of life, to mark particular occurrences.[7]

It's a beautiful image: those scraps of paper, or notebooks, filled with the feelings that you tried to make sense of and express in writing during difficult times – or even during good times. As someone who tries to make a habit of journal writing, the notion of words as 'pillars of witness' was always especially lovely to me. It emphasises the importance of those events and feelings you've tried to record; even once you have moved on, the proof that you experienced it remains, to remind you that you survived, or to reassure you that better times have happened and will happen again.

We can assume that Agnes's point of view here is also shared by Anne. But, you might ask, why is this acceptable, when we are warned of the dangers of interpreting fiction as autobiographical? Well, it takes a much smaller stretch of the imagination to believe that Anne held the same opinion that she gave to Agnes regarding poetry, than it does to suggest that a Gondal poem written from the point of view of an orphan is autobiographical.

When we consider Anne's reasons for writing, it makes sense that she should give some of her ideas and beliefs to her characters. But what *were* Anne's reasons for writing? We can find one answer in her preface to the second edition of *The Tenant of Wildfell Hall*:

> My object in writing the following pages, was not simply to amuse the Reader, neither was it to gratify my own taste, nor yet to ingratiate myself with the Press and the Public: I wished to tell the truth, for truth always conveys its own moral to those who are able to receive it. [...] I know that such characters do exist [see Arthur Huntingdon, Lady Lowborough, etc.], and if I have warned one rash youth from following in their steps, or prevented one thoughtless girl from falling into the very natural error of my heroine, the book has not been written in vain.[8]

Anne aimed to instruct and to give advice, with transparency and sincerity. Her non-Gondal poems were a way in which she could seek her own counsel, and work through her doubts and insecurities. Her novels expanded on this, taking her ideas and presenting them to anyone who wanted to read them.

Edward Chitham separated Anne's non-Gondal poems into two groups: 'religious and thoughtful poems' and 'dialogue and philosophical poems'.[9] It's the latter we're interested in here (see Chapter Five for the religious poetry) as these are the poems in which there are two or more voices, each presenting a point of view, who then spend the rest of the poem rationally discussing the subject until they reach a conclusion. This sounds like a pretty dry way to approach poetry, but thankfully for us, Anne manages to pull you in with her simple yet emotive language.

The three best examples of this style of poetry are Anne's longest non-Gondal poems, 'Views of Life', 'The Three Guides' and 'Self-Communion'. 'The Three Guides' is the most well known, having been picked up by critics in a way that many of her other poems were not, and it has also been anthologised.[10] All three poems represent an inner dialogue, between the narrator's differing feelings and points of view, and all move towards a hopeful conclusion about how the narrator should live to improve the lives of themselves and those around them. Self-improvement as the result of deep introspection is a recurring theme throughout Anne's work, and she seemed to have seen it as a general rule for life. If you can do something better, if you can improve yourself by some way and make others' lives easier, then do it.

'Views of Life' first appeared in the 1846 collection *Poems*, and it was completed while Anne was a governess at Thorp Green. The poem pits Hope against Experience – Experience implores Youth to ignore Hope completely, insisting that, in time, all experience will bring pain and to entertain hope is foolish. The poem begins with one of the best descriptions I've read of how easy it is for someone in the midst of despair to believe that *this* state is their true state; they have woken up, they 'know' that their negative view of life and of themselves is true:

When sinks my heart in hopeless gloom,
When life can shew no joy for me,
And I behold a yawning tomb
Where bowers and palaces should be,

In vain, you talk of morbid dreams,
In vain, you gaily smiling say
That what to me so dreary seems
The healthy mind deems bright and gay.

I too have smiled, and thought like you,
But madly smiled, and falsely deemed:
My present thoughts I know are true,
I'm waking now, 'twas then I dreamed.

The narrator spends the next few stanzas cynically describing how life 'looks fair and gay' under the 'false light' of youth. An example is given of a young mother and her new child: neither of them is aware of the horrors that wait for them. The child may die young, and even if he survives, he will have to see his mother die eventually. He cannot see how 'despairing and alone, / He then must wear his life away / And linger feebly toiling on, / And fainting sink into decay.'

Hope then makes its appearance to encourage the narrator that experience doesn't have to simply bring with it misery, but is interrupted by Experience, which begins to list its grievances against hope:

'O! heed her not,' experience says,
'For this she whispered once to me;
She told me in my youthful days
How glorious manhood's prime would be.

'When in the time of early Spring
Too chill the winds that o'er me passed,
She said each coming day would bring
A fairer heaven, a gentler blast.'

Summer comes around, and Experience complains of the 'scorching sky', which makes nature mourn the 'freshness of the spring'. Hope then tells Experience to wait for autumn, when the unbearable heat will die down. This exchange continues, until Experience claims that with winter comes the end of hope, implying that throughout the seasons of one's life, the things you hope to look forward to bring nothing but disappointment – there is no hope to be had.

The narrator takes Hope's side, telling Experience that it 'canst not quench the ardent fire / That warms the heart of youth'. The later part of the poem is more uplifting, urging travellers through life to notice those things that bring them joy, even when they are going through a difficult time, and hope will never leave them:

Because the road is rough and long,
Shall we despise the skylark's song,
    That cheers the wanderer's way?
Or trample down, with reckless feet
The smiling flowerets bright and sweet
    Because they soon decay?

Pass pleasant scenes unnoticed by,
Because the next is bleak and drear;
Or not enjoy a smiling sky
Because a tempest may be near?

No! while we journey on our way,
We'll notice every lovely thing,
And ever as they pass away,
To memory and hope we'll cling.[11]

The concept of paying attention to the small things, and finding happiness despite your circumstances, feels like a very modern way of thinking. Spend any amount of time on Facebook or Instagram and you'll come across inspirational quotes that remind you to take the time to stop and look around you, to 'be present in the moment'. It may sound trite when posted on social media, but it's an attitude that has been central to mindfulness and meditation for a long time. Anne's ability to present multiple arguments and come to a positive conclusion is indicative of her very organised mind; it's highly

'The Governess', by Emily Mary Osborn.

doubtful that she knew about the concept of mindfulness, but it's clear that she practised being present in her everyday life (pass by a pleasant scene and fail to notice it? No!).

'The Three Guides', written in 1847, sees the narrator torn between the philosophies of three spirits: earth, pride and faith. Each spirit takes up nine stanzas, during which the narrator argues with both earth and pride, and finally finds in faith a philosophy that she can agree with.

1

Spirit of earth! thy hand is chill.
I've felt its icy clasp;
And shuddering I remember still
That stony-hearted grasp.
Thine eye bids love and joy depart,
O turn its gaze from me!
It presses down my sinking heart;—
I will not walk with thee!

2

'Wisdom is mine,' I've heard thee say,
'Beneath my searching eye,
All mist and darkness melt away,
Phantoms and fables fly.
Before me, truth can stand alone,
The naked, solid truth;
And man matured my worth will own,
If I am shunned by youth.'

The spirit of earth boasts wisdom, telling the narrator that they can recognise the absolute truth in every situation. 'Phantoms and fables fly' says earth, implying that to follow earth's philosophy is to see everything starkly and plainly as it is, without imagination. The narrator does not want this, and tells the spirit of earth that she will not follow them because she values too much her ability of finding joy in the things around her. She also asserts that the spirit of earth is incapable of finding the best way through an obstacle when one appears in its path, and will instead try to boorishly plough through, with no tact and no thought given to alternative solutions:

9
Right through the flinty rock thou'll try
Thy toilsome way to bore,
Regardless of the pathway nigh
That would conduct thee o'er.
Not only art thou, then, unkind,
And freezing cold to me,
But unbelieving, deaf, and blind—
I will not walk with thee!

Pride is the second spirit to converse with the narrator, though it is less of a conversation than it is a string of insults aimed at the narrator once she says that she will not follow pride:

11
'Coward and fool!' thou mayst reply;
'Walk on the common sod;
Go trace, with timid foot and eye,
The steps by others trod.
'Tis best the beaten path to keep,
The ancient faith to hold,
To pasture with the fellow sheep,
And lie within the fold.

12

'Cling to the earth, poor grovelling worm,
'Tis not for thee to soar
Against the fury of the storm,
Amid the thunder's roar.
There's glory in that daring strife
Unknown, undreamt by thee;
There's speechless rapture in the life
Of those who follow me!'[12]

Pride does initially sound appealing: those who follow this spirit experience 'Ecstatic joys' and 'powers almost divine'. But the narrator sees through pride's boastfulness and deduces that it is superficial and will abandon its followers as soon as trouble appears. Not only that, but pride has a terrible temper. As soon as the narrator refused to follow pride, it became abusive: 'Bright as thou art, and bold, and strong, / That fierce glance wins not me, / And I abhor thy scoffing tongue —/ I will not walk with thee!'

The spirit of faith provides the narrator with a philosophy that she can believe in, and which balances both pride and earth. The final stanzas of the poem demonstrate how the narrator can avoid becoming hard-hearted while still being rational, and how she can take pride in her life without abandoning others and thinking herself too important.

'Self-Communion' is one of Anne's longest poems and was completed in April 1848. The dialogue in the poem takes place between the narrator and another figure referred to as 'pilgrim'. The narrator tries to encourage the pilgrim to take some rest, but the pilgrim responds that they cannot rest while time is passing by them so quickly and they have so much left to do. As in 'The Three Guides' the influence of the spirit of earth can be seen here again: 'I see that time, and toil, and truth / An inward hardness can impart,— / Can freeze the generous blood of youth, / And steel full fast the tender heart.' The pilgrim laments the sufferings they had to endure, as well as the suffering they have done on others' behalf.

The narrator of the poem listens to the pilgrim's struggles, and empathises with them, while trying to remind them that no matter how difficult life on Earth is and how much pain the pilgrim experiences, they have 'A lasting rest from pain and sin' to look forward to. That doesn't mean that the pilgrim will spend the rest of their life wishing for death, however. 'Rest *without* toil I would not ask' they say, knowing that all of the love and empathy they express during their life, while facing struggles and pain, will please their God more than if they were to give in to the spirit of earth and become hard of heart.

It may sound like a very conventional view, the Christian knowledge that there is a heaven to strive towards during their lifetime. And as readers in the present we are well aware that Anne died just over a year after writing this poem. I am thankful that I get to experience this poem, but when I read it, I find myself wishing that someone could have told her that she was doing more good than she realised, that she had less to worry about than she thought. But that is where part of Anne's power lies – without her faith, she could have easily succumbed to the despair that the pilgrim in the poem speaks of. The lure of the spirit of earth could have become too much for her without that conviction in her beliefs that encouraged her to continue to feel empathy even in the face of all her experiences.

One section of 'Self-Communion' has been taken as evidence of the growing emotional distance between Anne and Emily. About halfway through the poem, the pilgrim speaks about the joys of friendship. The pilgrim once experienced a wonderful early friendship that slowly became a source of sadness as the friends grew apart, and the pilgrim had to start keeping some of their thoughts and feelings to themselves when once they would have been able to tell the friend everything:

Oh, I have known a wondrous joy
In early friendship's pure delight,—
A genial bliss that could not cloy—
My sun by day, my moon by night.
Absence, indeed, was sore distress,
And thought of death was anguish keen,
And there was cruel bitterness
When jarring discords rose between;
And sometimes it was grief to know
My fondness was but half returned.
But this was nothing to the woe
With which another truth was learned:—
That I must check, or nurse apart
Full many an impulse of the heart
    And many a darling thought:
What my soul worshipped, sought and prized,
Were slighted, questioned, or despised;—
    This pained me more than aught.
And as my love the warmer glowed
The deeper would that anguish sink,
That this dark stream between us flowed,
Though both stood bending o'er its brink.
Until, at last, I learned to bear
A colder heart within my breast;
To share such thoughts as I could share,
    And calmly keep the rest.
I saw that they were sundered now,

The trees that at the root were one:
They yet might mingle leaf and bough,
But still the stems must stand alone.[13]

Both Edward Chitham and Samantha Ellis have written about the changing relationship between the two sisters, and their differing tastes and beliefs as they get older. To Anne it was important to live a life full of empathy, in which you use your talents and do everything within your power to help others and keep yourself healthy: 'To lighten woe, to trample sin, / And foes without and foes within / To combat and subdue.'[14] Emily seemed to have given up on the real world, instead preferring her imaginary world of Gondal. Samantha Ellis sums up this change in attitudes with great understanding: 'For Anne, imagination was a route to change in the real world. But Emily didn't feel the same way [...] Emily clung to imagination as an evasion of real life, a refusal. At twenty-six, in her poem "To Imagination", she rejected "the world without" as "hopeless", and pledged allegiance to "the world within". Anne often thought the world was a mess but she always had hope, always thought change was possible.'[15]

Anne's analytical mind was responsible for some of the most relatable poetry I've ever read. As someone who has been described as an incessant worrier, I can recognise in Anne's longer, self-reflective poems the need for an answer to big questions – how do I lead a life that benefits others as well as myself? How do I know if I'm doing a good job with my personal relationships? What do I do if the simple things that gave me joy don't give me joy any more? I might not be able to relate to Anne's faith, but I can appreciate her message of hope.

PASSIONATE POETRY

William Weightman, the popular curate at Haworth between 1839 and 1842, seemingly shared with Anne some of the values expressed in her 'pillars of witness' poems. Like her, Weightman spent his life in the service of others and trying to make their lives easier and better. But where Anne performed her duties with gravity and apparent seriousness, and kept to herself, Weightman's flamboyancy was hard not to notice. He was twenty-six when he arrived at the parsonage, bright, charming, and (if we believe Charlotte's portrait of him to be a true likeness) good-looking. There are two poems written by Anne that are often taken as evidence of her feelings for Weightman: 'Self-Congratulation', written about a month after Anne met him for the first time, and 'To —', written after his death.

'To —' begins as an address to someone who has presumably passed away. The narrator compares this person to a dazzling morning sun; the brighter and merrier that sun beam, the sooner it will fade and be replaced by clouds. It's Anne's take on the common saying that good people are taken too soon:

I will not mourn thee, lovely one,
    Though thou art torn away.
'Tis said that if the morning sun
    Arise with dazzling ray

And shed a bright and burning beam
    Athwart the glittering main,
'Ere noon shall fade that laughing gleam
    Engulfed in clouds and rain.

And if thy life as transient proved,
    It hath been full as bright,

For thou wert hopeful and beloved;
Thy spirit knew no blight.

If few and short the joys of life
That thou on earth couldst know,
Little thou knew't of sin and strife
Nor much of pain and woe.

If vain thy earthly hopes did prove,
Thou canst not mourn their flight;
Thy brightest hopes were fixed above
And they shall know no blight.

And yet I cannot check my sighs,
Thou wert so young and fair,
More bright than summer morning skies,
But stern death would not spare;

He would not pass our darling by
Nor grant one hour's delay,
But rudely closed his shining eye
And frowned his smile away,

That angel smile that late so much
Could my fond heart rejoice;
And he has silenced by his touch
The music of thy voice.

I'll weep no more thine early doom,
But O! I still must mourn
The pleasures buried in thy tomb,
For they will not return.[16]

When it comes to this poem, I think I agree with Juliet Barker more than I do with Edward Chitham: Anne was capable of writing passionate love stories in her Gondal poems, and this poem reads less like it was written by a mourning lover, and more like someone mourning the loss of a good friend and person, someone gone too young. There is the argument that perhaps she had to mask her emotions in order to hide her attachment to Weightman, but again, her dialogue and philosophical poems don't gloss over or hide anything. Anne wasn't afraid to write the truth – it was one of the aims of her writing, after all.

The second poem, 'Self-Congratulation', is more likely to be specifically about Weightman. It's another poem in which there are two speakers, the narrator and a supposed friend, who is asking about the narrator's sudden changes in behaviour. The narrator makes up an excuse about how 'childhood's thoughts are gone' and 'Each year its own new feelings brings', before congratulating themselves on being able to deceive those around them. The narrator then reveals the truth to the reader: they are in love, probably unrequited, and are trying their hardest to conceal this fact from everyone around them:

> I've noticed many a youthful form
> Upon whose changeful face
> The inmost workings of the soul
> The gazer's eye might trace.
> The speaking eye, the changing lip,
> The ready blushing cheek,
> The smiling or beclouded brow
> Their different feelings speak.

But, thank God! you might gaze on mine
    For hours and never know
The secret changes of my soul
    From joy to bitter woe.
Last night as we sat round the fire
    Conversing merrily,
We heard without approaching steps
    Of one well known to me.

There was no trembling in my voice,
    No blush upon my cheek,
No lustrous sparkle in my eyes
    Of hope or joy to speak.
But O my spirit burned within,
    My heart beat thick and fast.
He came not nigh—he went away
    And then my joy was past.

And yet my comrades marked it not,
    My voice was still the same;
They saw me smile, and o'er my face—
    No sign of sadness came;
They little knew my hidden thoughts
    And they will never know
The anguish of my drooping heart,
    The bitter aching woe![17]

Both Samantha Ellis and Edward Chitham believe this was written about Weightman, with Ellis writing that:

> It is typical of reserved Anne that the first poem she (probably) wrote about Weightman isn't about being in

> love but about how to hide it. […] I think Anne liked and wanted Weightman, but she could also see he was an incorrigible charmer; and, perhaps, before giving him her heart, she wanted to see if he'd grow up.'[18]

But Juliet Barker suggests that the whole situation was a flirtation and nothing more, and she makes the astute point that if any kind of relationship had developed then 'Charlotte would have been the first to comment on it.'[19]

Whatever your opinion may be on Anne's relationship with Weightman, I think it's unfair that her poetry should be reduced to whether or not it was about someone she may have been in love with. 'Self-Congratulation', though it has a Gondal signature, marks Anne's move towards more personal poems. It is the first example of a more personal poem by Anne that exists, and it provides the reader with significant clues about how Anne faced the world. She was twenty in 1840 and had already learned to take pride in being able to hide her feelings, even from those closest to her. 'Self-Communion', written eight years later, is much more self-aware and tells us a bit about why she felt that she had to hide her real self. But 'Self-Congratulation' lets the reader know that when it comes to Anne Brontë, there is more than just what there appears to be on the surface.

My favourite example of this is related to the assumption that Anne was the least ambitious of the sisters, quietly presenting her poems to the pushier Charlotte. But Anne was the only Brontë sister to independently send a poem to a magazine and see it published. In August 1848, *Fraser's Magazine* printed 'The Three Guides'. They published another of her poems that December, 'The Narrow Way'.[20] Ellen was visiting Haworth at that time, to comfort the family after Emily's death. She noticed

Anne reading a magazine and watched 'a gentle smile of pleasure stealing over her placid face as she read. "What is the matter?" asked the friend. "Why do you smile?" "Only because I see they have inserted one of my poems," was the quiet reply. And not a word more was said on the subject.'[21]

AGNES GREY

After the publication of *Poems* in 1846 with its terrible sales and lacklustre reviews, Anne, Emily and Charlotte began putting together their first novels. The apparent failure of their collection of poetry seems not to have fazed them, but instead to spur them on to achieve their literary goals.

When Currer Bell's *Jane Eyre* began to cause a sensation, the publisher Thomas Cautley Newby realised that he could potentially make money from the two other Bell novels. But Newby proved to be an unreliable and opportunistic publisher. First, Anne and Emily had to pay fifty pounds, which would be refunded if and when their novels sold enough copies to cover the advance.[22] Second, when *Wuthering Heights* and *Agnes Grey* were finally published in December 1847, Anne and Emily discovered, to their horror, that none of the corrections that they had made to the proofs had been included in the published books.[23]

Charlotte's book was being criticised for its 'low tone of behaviour'[24], and the publication of *Wuthering Heights* and *Agnes Grey* gave more fuel to the critics who were already unimpressed by Currer Bell's characters and choice of subject matter: 'In each, there is the autobiographical form of writing; a choice of subjects that are peculiar without being either probable or pleasing; and considerable executive ability, but insufficient to overcome the injudicious selection of the theme and matter.'[25]

Almost as soon as the Brontës' first novels were published, the comparisons started. A long tradition of comparing Anne unfavourably to her sisters began when reviewers started to gloss over *Agnes Grey*, comparing it to *Wuthering Heights* and finding that Anne's novel lacked the power of Emily's and was, on the whole, more agreeable in tone. 'Some characters and scenes are nicely sketched in it but it has nothing to call for a special notice,' was the conclusion of the *Britannia*. The *Atlas* was even more damning and described *Agnes Grey* as 'a somewhat coarse imitation of one of Miss Austin's [sic] charming stories [...] it leaves no painful impression on the mind – some may think it leaves no impression at all.'[26]

Even the more favourable reviews compared Anne's work to that of her sisters. '*Agnes Grey* is a tale well worth the writing and the reading. The heroine is a sort of younger sister to Jane Eyre; but inferior to her in every way.'[27] The comparison with *Jane Eyre* was particularly unfair – Anne had completed her novel about the life of a governess before Charlotte had written *Jane Eyre*. If *Agnes Grey* had been published first, it may eventually have been compared to *Jane Eyre*, but at least it would have had the chance to be the first novel to feature a plain heroine, a governess, and a critical view of the options open to women who wished to earn their own living.

Agnes Grey is, essentially, a story about work. Agnes is the youngest daughter of a clergyman and his wife and is well aware that she will need to be able to earn her own living eventually. Much to the surprise of the rest of her family, she expresses a desire to become a governess. Agnes finds herself a position with the Bloomfield family but lasts less than a year after she has great difficulty disciplining her pupils. Her second governess position is much more successful, and she remains with the Murray family until the death of her father. Agnes then returns to her mother, and together they start their own successful school. While the plot is fairly simple, Agnes's navigation of the trials and challenges she faces are far from it. While dealing with the difficulties of her position as a governess and what that means about her social standing, Agnes experiences love, which she assumes is unrequited.

While a governess, Agnes has little to no autonomy when it comes to her free time; she is constantly at the mercy of her pupils, Rosalie and Matilda Murray. The concept of work–life balance did not exist for people in Anne's position, which was that of servitude to a wealthy family. In her introduction to the Everyman's Library edition of *Agnes Grey* and *The Tenant of Wildfell Hall*, Lucy Hughes-Hallett writes about *Agnes Grey*: 'It is that rare thing, a novel about work. It examines – as fiction rarely does – relations between employers and employees, and it does so through a sequence of vividly dramatic scenes.'[28]

One of the most powerful passages in the book occurs when Agnes is contemplating how she herself is changing as a result of her working environment. She has just spent some of her precious free time with good company, speaking about

'Bowles Drawing Book for Ladies; or Complete Florist': An 'accomplishments' manual for young women of leisure.

issues that are important to her. She even got to speak about Mr Weston, the curate, without making her feelings about him obvious. On the way home, she thinks about how nice it is to speak to people sympathetic to her own character, then moves into more melancholy thoughts about loneliness. It is quoted at length here because the points that Anne makes are still relatable today:

> In returning to the lodge, I felt very happy, and thanked God that I had now something to think about, something to dwell on as a relief from the weary monotony, the lonely drudgery of my present life – for I *was* lonely – never, from month to month, from year to year, except during my brief intervals of rest at home, did I see one creature to whom I could open my heart, or freely speak my thoughts with any hope of sympathy, or even comprehension; [...] My only companions had been unamiable children, and ignorant, wrong-headed girls, from whose fatiguing folly, unbroken solitude was often a relief most earnestly desired and dearly prized. But to be restricted to such associates was a serious evil, both in its immediate effects and the consequences that were likely to ensue.
>
> Never a new idea or a stirring thought came to me from without; and such as rose within me were, for the most part, miserably crushed at once, or doomed to sicken and fade away, because they could not see the light.
>
> Habitual associations are known to exercise great influence over each other's minds and manners. Those whose actions are for ever before our eyes, whose words are ever in our ears, will naturally lead us, albeit against our will – slowly – gradually – imperceptibly, perhaps, to act and speak as they do. [...] And I, as I could not make

> my young companions better, feared exceedingly that they would make me worse – would gradually bring my feelings, habits, capacities, to the level of their own [...] Already, I seemed to feel my intellect deteriorating, my heart petrifying, my soul contracting, and I trembled lest my very moral perceptions should become deadened, my distinctions of right and wrong confounded, and all my better faculties be sunk, at last, beneath the baleful influence of such a mode of life.[29]

Anyone who has found themselves in a job that they don't enjoy, that doesn't challenge them, or in which they feel lonely, can find some sympathy in Agnes's melancholic train of thought. My newsfeed often throws out articles about how loneliness is on the rise: the work–life balance is more lop-sided than ever; people are working longer hours in multiple jobs; lots of us are working from home and don't make contact with others for days at a time. Olivia Laing's book *The Lonely City* charts her journey to make sense of the loneliness she was feeling when she moved to New York; like Agnes, she doesn't shy away from the feeling and instead examines it closely, making sure that she doesn't lose herself in her surroundings: 'What does it mean to be lonely? How do we live, if we're not intimately engaged with another human being? How do we connect with other people, especially if we don't find speaking easy?'[30]

Agnes is often spoken for, rather than being asked her opinion. She is, as a result, unfairly represented, particularly by Rosalie Murray, her eldest pupil. In one scene, Rosalie and Matilda have returned home after meeting Mr Weston, the object of Agnes's affection. The two girls (mainly Rosalie) up until this point have been preventing Agnes from attending church or visiting the cottages, out of a kind of bored, vindictive cruelty. They know she wants to meet Mr Weston, and so they give her large amounts of boring, time-consuming work to do. They relate to Agnes what they have said to Mr Weston about her:

> 'He wondered why you were never with us, and thought you must have delicate health, as you came out so seldom.'
>
> 'He didn't, Matilda – what nonsense you're talking!'
>
> 'Oh, Rosalie, what a lie! He did, you know [...] And, Miss Grey, Rosalie told him you were quite well, but you were always so buried in your books that you had had no pleasure in anything else.'
>
> 'What an idea he must have of me!' I thought.
>
> 'And,' I asked, 'does old Nancy ever inquire about me?'
>
> 'Yes, and we tell her that you are so fond of reading and drawing that you can do nothing else.'
>
> 'That is not the case though; if you had told her I was so busy I *could* not come to see her, it would have been nearer the truth.'
>
> 'I don't think it would,' replied Miss Murray, suddenly kindling up; 'I'm sure you have plenty of time to yourself now, when you have so little teaching to do.'
>
> It was no use beginning to dispute with such indulged, unreasoning creatures; so I held my peace. I was accustomed, now, to keeping silence when things distasteful to my ear were uttered; and now, too, I was used to wearing a placid smiling countenance when my heart was bitter within me. Only those who have felt the like can imagine my feelings, as I sat with an assumption of smiling indifference [...][31]

Agnes's attitude echoes the narrator in 'Self-Congratulation' – instead of making her feelings known, she suppresses them. She knows that she won't get anywhere with Rosalie and Matilda, and if she argues with them, she may end up dropping down to their level. Which is what she feared would happen.

The similarity to 'Self-Congratulation', and some of Anne's other 'pillars of witness', can lead us to the conclusion that *Agnes Grey* is heavily autobiographical. Winifred Gérin takes this view to the extreme, possibly based on Charlotte's comment to Elizabeth Gaskell that *Agnes Grey* was 'the novel in which her sister Anne pretty literally describes her own experience as a governess'.[32] Charlotte's simplistic view yet again shows just how much she underestimated the capabilities of her youngest sister.

Agnes's experiences do shadow some of Anne's experiences: two posts as a governess, one that is more successful than the other. However, if the book *was* just a literal reproduction of Anne's time as a governess, it would not be half as readable as it is. The critic Stevie Davies makes the important point that 'Anne worked *from* autobiographical material rather than in servitude to it [...] The genuineness of texture and dialogue in *Agnes Grey* is the product of minute observation, focused by a fine authorial irony and delicate power of understatement.'[33]

So what is the autobiographical material that Anne worked from? When thinking about how work is portrayed in the book, especially women's work, it's important to note that Agnes chose to work, rather than working out of necessity. She shocked her family, just as Anne did, by wanting to find a governess position. Both Anne and Agnes are the babies of their families, so it's reasonable to assume that Agnes's feelings of wanting to prove herself to her family are based on the same feelings that Anne had:

> 'But mamma, I am above eighteen, and quite able to take care of myself, and others too. You do not know half the wisdom and prudence I possess, because I have never been tried.'
>
> 'Only think,' said Mary, 'what would you do in a house full of strangers, without me or mamma to speak and act for you... with a parcel of children, besides yourself, to attend to; and no one to look to for advice? You would not even know what clothes to put on.'
>
> 'You think, because I always do as you bid me, I have no judgement of my own: but only try me – that is all I ask – and you shall see what I can do.'[34]

Agnes's life bears some other similarities to Anne's: they both have a clergyman father, and they both have comparable experiences as governesses. But Agnes is not Anne. Anne gave some of her ideals and beliefs to Agnes, and she used Agnes to tell a story very different to her own life. In doing so, she created a very relatable heroine who expressed herself clearly and sincerely. By drawing on her own experiences, she created a believable and honest look at the life of a governess in the nineteenth century. Lady Amberley, a Victorian suffragist, wrote in her diary that she 'should like to give [*Agnes Grey*] to every family with a governess and shall read it through again when I have a governess to remind me to be human.'[35]

The character of Mr Edward Weston is often another subject of scrutiny when considering *Agnes Grey* as an autobiographical novel. It's a popular belief that Anne based Weston on her father's curate, William Weightman. Yes, both were curates, and both were favourites with the local parishioners, but the resemblances end there. Daphne du Maurier wrote a perceptive criticism of the suggestion that Edward Weston is

William Weightman, pointing out that 'the grave, quiet, plain Mr. Weston of *Agnes Grey* bears small resemblance to the gay, flirtatious, light-hearted "Celia Amelia" of Charlotte's letters.'[36]

Her defence of Anne and her capacity for imagination continues, and she makes the point that the Robinsons, often cited as the inspiration for the Murrays, cannot have been as 'rude, shallow, uncultured and disagreeable' as Agnes's employers: 'Anne was a young woman of spirit and determination. She would never have endured the insults and slights that Mrs. Murray and her daughter Rosalie put upon Agnes Grey, nor would she have encouraged a brother who had already lost one position as tutor to take up another with people of no integrity.'[37]

One final aspect to consider about Agnes Grey is the fact that it's just so readable. Anne's emotional intelligence creates psychologically true characters who pull you in to their everyday lives. It's true that, in terms of plot, not very much happens. But for the reader, this sparseness of plot is somehow irresistible. Anne's prose is deceptively simple, and simplicity often leads people to believe that, for some reason, the prose itself is not literary.

The readability debate is something that has been going on for a long time. Does writing have to be complex to be considered literary? Can a bestseller be literary? A bestseller implies a book that is very readable to a wide variety of people, which, for some reason, has come to be equated with non-literary fiction. Readability somehow implies a lack of abstraction and imagination. But in *Agnes Grey*, Anne has created a layered story. Underneath the readability – the simple, beautiful prose – is a subtle undercurrent of Anne's views on society, work and the limited options available to women of the time. George Moore praised *Agnes Grey* as 'the most perfect prose narrative in English letters.'[38] Stevie Davies took this further, with the most fitting description of *Agnes Grey* that I have so far read: 'The novel, read sympathetically, has the beauty and sadness of music scored in a minor key.'[39]

THE TENANT OF WILDFELL HALL

> Ever since the completion of Anne Brontë's tale of *Agnes Grey*, she had been labouring at a second, *The Tenant of Wildfell Hall*. It is little known; the subject – the deterioration of a character, whose profligacy and ruin took their rise in habits of intemperance, so slight as to be only considered 'good fellowship' – was painfully discordant to one who would fain have sheltered herself from all but peaceful and religious ideas.[40]

Anne's most notorious/derided/obscure/revolutionary work has, from the start, been referred to as a mistake. Charlotte began the trend in her 'Biographical Notice', and her thoughts were echoed by Mrs Gaskell (see the quote above). Ultimately, the novel was unfairly dismissed for over a century (see also Chapter Three).

In an amazing feat of productivity, Anne's second novel was published in June 1848 by Thomas Cautley Newby, just six months after *Agnes Grey*. It was immediately met with accusations of crudeness and vulgarity, following the same vein as the previous reviews of books by the Bells. *The Spectator* was especially critical:

> *The Tenant of Wildfell Hall*, like its predecessor, suggests the idea of considerable abilities ill applied. There is power, effect, and even nature, though of an extreme kind, in its pages; but there seems in the writer a morbid love for the coarse, not to say the brutal; so that his level

> subjects are not very attractive, and the more forcible are displeasing or repulsive, from their gross, physical, or profligate substratum [...] There is a coarseness of tone throughout the writing of all these Bells, that puts an offensive subject in its worst point of view, and which generally contrives to dash indifferent things.[41]

Why was there such a backlash? Why did even Charlotte refer to her sister's novel as a 'complete mistake'?

The Tenant of Wildfell Hall tells the story of a 'fallen woman'. Helen Graham makes the mistake of marrying Arthur Huntingdon, a man who at first appears charming and handsome. Her aunt advises against the match, but Helen, naïvely thinking that she can change him and help him to become a better man, goes against her aunt's wishes and marries him anyway. We then follow the deterioration of their marriage in painful detail. Arthur's decline into alcoholism coincides with the birth and early childhood of her son. She asks Arthur for a separation, and requests that he let her and her small son leave. Arthur refuses, and so Helen forms a plan to leave. She takes her son and escapes to Wildfell Hall, where we meet her at the beginning of the book.

Helen's story unfolds in the form of a diary. Helen gives her diary to Gilbert Markham, to try to explain her situation to him. In Gilbert's village, Helen is considered odd and unorthodox: rumours abound about her previous life (she presents herself as a widow and goes by her maiden name). Helen and Gilbert eventually fall in love, but can only be together once Helen's husband has died – much like Jane in *Jane Eyre*, she refuses to be a mistress and returns to her dying husband out of both duty and a strong sense of empathy. After the death of Arthur, Helen returns to Wildfell Hall and is reunited with Gilbert.

When Anne wrote the book, Helen's actions were against the law. *Wildfell Hall*, like *Agnes Grey*, is a harsh critique of the options that were open to women of the time, when getting married was really the only acceptable occupation. If you couldn't do that, then your life would be full of uncertainty. Anne, however, gave Helen a means of making a living – she is a painter who sells her work. *Wildfell Hall* is also a critique of women's rights, especially when it came to marriage and abusive partners (see Chapter Six).

Anne handles the serious issues that *Wildfell Hall* tackles in a sensitive and sympathetic way. The first time the reader meets Helen, she is presented as an outsider – the residents of the village take great pleasure in dissecting her character, and Gilbert does not like her as she makes her (very odd) opinions known and does not defer to men who may have a different opinion. Framing Helen in this way allows the reader to get to know her at the same pace as Gilbert, with her personality slowly emerging as she learns to trust that Gilbert is not like her husband.

PRELUDES.

I.

The Wife's Tragedy.

MAN must be pleased ; but him to please
Is woman's pleasure ; down the gulf
Of his condoled necessities
She casts her best, she flings herself.
How often flings for nought ! and yokes
Her heart to an icicle or whim,
Whose each impatient word provokes
Another, not from her, but him ;
While she, too gentle even to force
His penitence by kind replies,

'An Angel in the House', Coventry Patmore's poem idealising women.

The book is told through a series of letters, from Gilbert to his friend Halford. The letters are eventually replaced by Helen's diary, which is where Gilbert, Halford and the reader learn about Helen's past and begin to understand her current position. The outsider with the strange opinions suddenly becomes a figure to admire and empathise with. There is a definite tonal shift too, between Gilbert's letters and Helen's diary – the story moves from being a satirical Jane Austen-style comedy of manners to a gothic tragedy. The shift is unexpected and quickly moves the reader into the dark and lonely world of Helen when she was Huntingdon's wife and prisoner. This method of getting the reader to empathise with Helen without even realising that we are doing so allows Anne to then expand on the issues she was passionate about: education, women's rights, abusive partners and the failures of the law in such cases, and a world in which people like Arthur Huntingdon are set up to fall (see Chapter Six for a more detailed look at Anne's social conscience).

Biographers and critics have often tried to suggest that Anne based Arthur Huntingdon solely on her brother Branwell and his decline into alcohol and opiate abuse. Again, this dismissed Anne's powerful imagination and, as Winifred Gérin points out, completely misses the point that Anne was trying to make, namely to condemn 'a world in which innocence, her brother's innocence as well as her own, is exposed to temptations so beyond their experience as to make havoc of conventional precept and virtue'. *Wildfell Hall* is 'not merely the story of Branwell's downfall, but of the world that made such a downfall possible'.[42]

There are many positive character traits that Branwell possessed and which Huntingdon does not: he was a hard worker; he felt remorse when he did wrong; and, most importantly, he loved and respected the women in his life.

If Branwell is like anyone in *Wildfell Hall*, it is Lord Lowborough, a friend of Huntingdon's. Lowborough, though easily tempted into bad habits, often tries to redeem himself. With much hard work, he manages to first stop gambling and then drinking. He decides that he needs to change, and tries, to the best of his ability, to do so. To this end, he marries Annabella Wilmot, thinking that the love of such a good and beautiful woman will help him to better himself. Annabella marries Lord Lowborough, but only for his title; she manages to deceive everyone, and later has an affair with Arthur Huntingdon. Over the course of the book, the reader comes to sympathise with Lowborough – his attempts to improve himself, his love for his wife, and his increased refusal to join in with the debauchery of his friends slowly endears him to the reader, until the betrayal of his deceptive wife firmly cements him as a character to be pitied.

Branwell's sisters believed his tale of an affair with Mrs Robinson, and blamed her for Branwell's demise, particularly after they received the news that Mrs Robinson had remarried after the death of her husband. They accused her of seducing Branwell only to discard him as soon as she was discovered. In this sense, Branwell's plight more strongly resembles that of Lord Lowborough than it does of the thoroughly unlikeable Arthur Huntingdon.

AUTOBIOGRAPHICAL ANNE?

Reading some of Anne's work as autobiographical can help us to understand her and how she lived her life, but it does need to be approached with caution. Poems like 'Self-Congratulation' have been used as proof of her feelings for William Weightman, but what often gets glossed over is its depiction of how someone can keep their inner life a complete secret even from those closest to them. If there's anything to take away from 'Self-Congratulation', it's not that Anne was secretly in love with Weightman, it's that Anne knew how to keep things to herself, even strong feelings that are hard to hide.

She knew what it was like to be talked over and completely ignored, and she understood loneliness, just like Agnes did. She could observe people, and mix everything she learned into three-dimensional, believable characters. The famous piece of advice that is often given to writers is 'write what you know' – but that doesn't just mean that you stick to your own

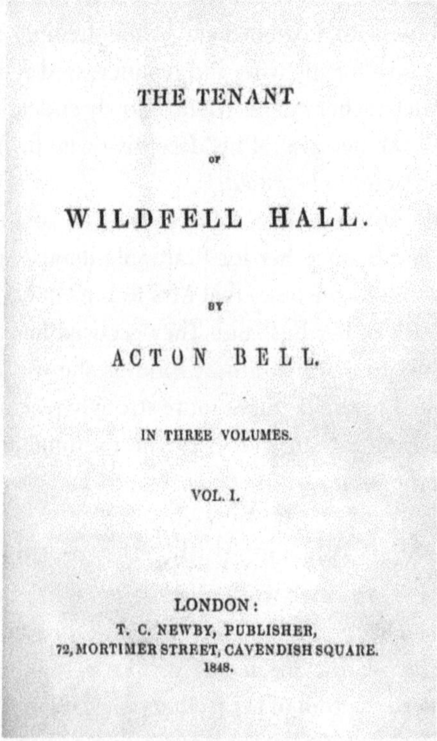

THE TENANT

OF

WILDFELL HALL.

BY

ACTON BELL.

IN THREE VOLUMES.

VOL. I.

LONDON:
T. C. NEWBY, PUBLISHER,
72, MORTIMER STREET, CAVENDISH SQUARE.
1848.

Title page of the first edition of Anne's groundbreaking novel.

experiences and the people who inhabit your life; it serves more as an encouragement to pay attention. Which is another thing that we know that Anne was good at, from poems like 'Views of Life', in which she urges the reader to notice every pleasant thing that they can, to acknowledge difficulties and sadness, and still move on.

While a governess at Thorp Green, Anne had plenty of opportunity to observe the family of her employer. And not just the family – she would have met friends and acquaintances of the Robinsons, at church, in Scarborough, at Thorp Green itself. All these observations found their way into *Wildfell Hall* in the habits and actions of the wealthy characters, with different personalities taken apart and built back up into new characters. It's true that part of the reason we interpret Anne's work as autobiographical is because we have so few of her personal writings. Another reason is the believability of the characters and scenarios she wrote about. But saying that Huntingdon just *has* to be based on Branwell insults Anne's imagination. She is often described as the least imaginative of the Brontës, possibly because her sisters' works are so fantastical and almost beyond reality. Anne's books are no less imaginative for being firmly placed in recognisable settings, and it is the power of her imagination that allowed her to build up those recognisable settings in the first place.

When thinking about Anne in particular, it's important to remember that although both of her books are written in the first person, the narrator's voice is not necessarily Anne's voice. In any book, there is the author (the actual person who wrote the sentences) and there is the narrator (the voice doing the storytelling) and they will often be different. Philip Pullman has written extensively about narrative voice, and he identifies one other person hanging about in this set-up: the 'implied author', the person the reader assumes is behind the book. The 'implied author', also described as the 'inferred author', is a combination of all the literary skills, the life experiences, the opinions and attitudes of the real author. It represents just one version of the author, and can be interpreted differently depending on the reader.

When we assume that *Agnes Grey* is entirely autobiographical, we are equating the narrator (Agnes) with the actual author (Anne), perhaps wrongly. But when we acknowledge that there are autobiographical elements, and also that these are exaggerated and fictionalised, the closest we can get to Anne is Pullman's 'implied author'. When it comes to the Brontës, Anne and Emily especially, the implied author is the closest we can ever get to really understanding who they were as people. As much as they fascinate us, as much as we would like to think we understand their personalities, they will always be 'the figure felt by the reader to lie behind the book'.[43]

THREE

Wildfell Hall

ANNE EDITED

When reading any kind of book, it's very easy to forget about all the other people who aren't the author but who were also involved in bringing the book into existence. Editors seem to disappear, and their influences on books are mostly forgotten. But this is the point of editing – a good editor will be able to make and suggest necessary changes to a book while retaining the author's voice and originality. In contrast, of course, some editors might alter a work so substantially as to lessen or even negate its intended impact. Anne Brontë edited her own work as she wrote, but people close to her also played a role.

The poems written by Anne that appear in the joint publication *Poems* were edited by both Anne and Charlotte, and it isn't unreasonable to imagine that Emily was involved too. And, considering the stories of how closely they worked together, it's easy to imagine them reading each other's works and providing criticism and feedback. There is also definite evidence that Charlotte edited Anne and Emily's poems and novels after their deaths.

One of the most significant edits of Anne's works was the 1854 *Parlour Library* edition of *The Tenant of Wildfell Hall*. The novel was altered almost beyond recognition, with multiple changes made that had a hugely detrimental effect. What was the nature of the changes? How did they affect the impact of the novel? And most importantly, how has this edition of *Wildfell Hall* affected Anne's reputation as a writer?

But Anne isn't just the victim of bad textual editors. In her 'Biographical Notice' featured in the 1850 edition of *Wuthering Heights* and *Agnes Grey*, Charlotte edited the details of her sisters' lives in order to protect them from the criticisms they were receiving from the general public and critics alike; criticisms that the deceased Anne and Emily could no longer defend against for themselves. The imagined version of Anne's character presented by Charlotte in this 'Biographical Notice' has persisted for almost as long as the bad editions of *Wildfell Hall*, and the combination of the two provided the public with a very unflattering image of Anne as both a person and a writer. This image of Anne snowballed into the one that is the most widely known today: that of the poor, shy, frail little girl who suffered from religious melancholy and who hid herself from the world behind 'a sort of nun-like veil, which was rarely lifted'.[1]

In the last chapter, I made the point that it is unwise to make assumptions about Anne's life based on her writing. Now I hope to show how the editing of Anne's works led to assumptions about her skill and ability as a writer, as well as looking at how her character and personality have been presented over the last two centuries.

A MANGLED TEXT

As discussed above, a good editor can help turn an ordinary book into something remarkable. A bad editor can have the opposite effect, which is what happened to *The Tenant of Wildfell Hall*. But what was so bad about the 1854 version of the text that future critics described it as mangled? And how did such a terrible version end up being published?

When *Wildfell Hall* was first published, the reaction of the general public was one of shock. Its notoriety resulted in a second edition, published with a new preface by Anne, in which she deftly and tactfully defended herself against accusations of coarseness and vulgarity. Anne fully acknowledges that both *Agnes Grey* and *Wildfell Hall* present unpalatable truths that the reader may find unpleasant, but that is the most important thing about them – they may be unpalatable but they are truths. She apologises for the places in which she may have gone too far, but still is able to justify her authorial decisions:

> [...] when we have to do with vice and vicious characters, I maintain it is better to depict them as they really are than as they would wish to appear. To represent a bad thing in its least offensive light is doubtless the most agreeable course for a writer of fiction to pursue; but is it the most honest, or the safest? Is it better to reveal the snares and pitfalls of life to the young and thoughtless traveller, or to cover them with branches and flowers? O Reader! if there were less of this delicate concealment of facts – this whispering 'Peace, peace,' when there is no peace – there would be less of sin and misery to the young of both sexes who are left to wring their bitter knowledge from experience.[2]

Throughout the preface Anne stresses how important it was for her to write truthful portrayals of unsavoury characters, stripping them of any romanticism they may be treated with by other authors. There is no happy ending for Helen and Arthur Huntingdon: *Wildfell Hall* turns on its head the notion that reformed rakes make the best husbands. And it does so very explicitly.

Anne stood by her novel and the choices she had made while writing it. Charlotte appears not to have agreed, however, and when her publisher approached Charlotte with the idea of republishing her sisters' novels after their deaths, she implied that *Wildfell Hall* should not be included as its subject matter was so in contrast to the character of the 'gentle, retiring, inexperienced writer' who wrote the book as if 'accomplishing a painful penance and a severe duty'.[3]

Charlotte readily agreed to the joint republication of *Agnes Grey* and *Wuthering Heights*, and it was in that edition's 'Biographical Notice of Ellis and Acton Bell' that Charlotte made clear what she thought of Anne's second novel: '*The Tenant of Wildfell Hall*, by Acton Bell, had likewise an unfavourable reception. At this I cannot wonder. The choice of subject was an entire mistake. Nothing less congruous with the writer's nature could be conceived.'[4] Charlotte's dismissal of *Wildfell Hall* in such a manner effectively suppressed the original text of *Wildfell Hall* until interest in Anne began to increase in the 1960s and '70s, at least in the UK. The American publisher of *Wildfell Hall*, Harper of New York, kept the original text in print, though without Anne's preface.[5]

By 1854, the Brontës' works were incredibly popular, but *Wildfell Hall* still had not been republished. The only versions available were the expensive three-volume editions published by Newby in 1848. The publisher Thomas Hodgson saw an opportunity to republish a cheap single-volume edition of *Wildfell Hall* as part of the *Parlour Library* series, to try and reach a wider market. Condensing a three-volume edition into one volume meant there had to be some alterations. The page layouts were changed in order to fit more text onto the page, but large edits still had to be carried out to make the text short enough to fit into this pocket-size edition. This is where the most significant damage took place. In the 1996 Penguin Classics edition of *Wildfell Hall*, the editor Stevie Davies notes that the text in the1854 *Parlour Library* edition is 'corrupt', 'highly expurgated' and 'would become the basis for most subsequent British editions. It is worthless to the modern editor.'[6]

It may be worthless when preparing a new edition of Anne's work, but in terms of Anne's literary reputation, looking at this 'corrupt text' can help us to see the damaging influence it had.

In *Take Courage: Anne Brontë and the Art of Life*, Samantha Ellis writes that her experience of comparing the heavily edited *Parlour Library* edition with the original Newby edition was 'infuriating', and she becomes convinced that the altered 1854 edition 'helps explain why [Anne's] work has been undervalued'.[7]

What could an editor possibly do to create such a terrible edition? Writing in the 1970s, G.D. Hargreaves listed some of the differences between the Newby edition and the 1854 edition. First, the opening section of the novel – Gilbert Markham's introductory letter to his friend J. Halford, Esq – is omitted in the later edition.[8]

Excluding this first letter to Halford completely changes the structure of the text, and it is never made apparent to the reader that the novel is framed as two letters, both written by Gilbert to his friend and brother-in-law J. Halford. There are other references to Halford throughout the book, mostly when Gilbert asks him a question about the events he has just set down on paper. Without the initial letter to open the novel the mentions of Halford can appear confusing, coming across as bad, lazy writing.

One of the biggest effects of the removal of the letter is that we lose the fact that Gilbert is writing his letters a long time in the future. Gilbert writes in his opening letter about their ages and the length of their friendship: '[…] at your age, and when we have known each other so long, […]'; and about 'musty old letters' and 'a certain faded old journal of mine' that will help him to write down 'an old world story', 'a full and faithful account of certain circumstances connected with the most important event of my life'.[9]

J. Halford is also the husband of Gilbert's younger sister Rose, who is nineteen at the beginning of the novel. Without the opening letter, we lose the context of Rose and Halford's long and presumably happy marriage, which is the reason Gilbert and Halford became friends in the first place. There are references to Rose throughout the book that take on more meaning when placed in the context of her future marriage, including some of Anne's feminist commentary on the expected subservience of daughters and sisters to their fathers and brothers.

Hargreaves also noted the removal of chapter headings and most of the italics from the *Parlour Library* edition of *Wildfell Hall*. This will most likely have been for cost reasons – removing chapter headings freed up more space on the page, and meant less type had to be set. Removing the italic type would have saved a lot of time, as the typesetters would not have had to leave their work to go set italic type from different drawers.[10] Anne made prominent use of italics throughout *Wildfell Hall* to denote sarcasm, and also to stress certain words or phrases. The loss of italics in most cases makes those sections more ambiguous, the original meaning being lost. Hargreaves uses the first meeting between Gilbert and Helen after Gilbert has read Helen's diary to illustrate how the removal of the italics in the *Parlour Library* edition significantly weakened the effect of the scene:

> 'Have you looked it over?' she murmured. The spell was broken.
>
> 'I've read it through,' said I, advancing into the room, – 'and I want to know if you'll forgive me – if you *can* forgive me?'
>
> She did not answer, but her eyes glistened, and a faint red mantled on her lip and cheek. As I approached, she abruptly turned away, and went to the window. It was not in anger, I was all assured, but only to conceal or control her emotion. I therefore ventured to follow and stand beside her there, – but not to speak. She gave me her hand, without turning her head, and murmured, in a voice she strove in vain to steady, –
>
> 'Can *you* forgive *me*?'[11]

Similarly, when Helen first learns of her husband's affair with Annabella, the wife of Lord Lowborough, she is understandably upset and avoids that evening's dinner, instead retiring to write down the events of the day to help compose her mind. But when she reminds herself that her unwelcome guests will still be there next morning her anger appears once again: 'I wish this day were over! I shudder at the thought of going down to breakfast – How shall I encounter them all? – Yet let me remember it is not *I* that am guilty: *I* have no cause to fear; and if *they* scorn me as the victim of their guilt, I can pity their folly and despise their scorn.'[12]

Taking away the italics from Helen's words partially removes the sense of fury that goes with them It makes the words feel cold and distant, dissociating them from the strong feelings that Helen has. The extra stress on the words *I* and *them* emphasises how different Helen feels from her husband and his associates; Helen here is recognising the distance between them rather than trying to tolerate her guests for the sake of her husband.

Free online versions of *Wildfell Hall* often do away with the italics entirely. The emphasis italics place on certain words in the dialogue of the novel are a mark of Anne's astute skills of observation – reading the dialogue aloud, complete with the italics, allows you to hear how natural Anne's dialogue is in both *Wildfell Hall* and *Agnes Grey*. Characters speak in a way that is natural to them and fitting for their personalities.

In the 1854 edition, the removal of chapter headings and italics still wasn't enough to reduce the text significantly enough, and so the text itself had to be cut further. Hargreaves writes that the longest omissions occur mostly in the chapters devoted to Helen's diary, and though it is not possible to know their reasons for removing certain passages, Hargreaves says that a sense of propriety combined with the need to save space may be responsible. Since Helen's diary contains some of the more controversial passages in the book, this is easy to believe. He writes that almost the entire 28th chapter ('Parental Feelings') has been removed, possibly out of a sense of 'family propriety', as this is the chapter in which Helen writes about her fears for her son's future, and her husband's worrying attitudes towards him.

The changes made to this chapter really are extreme.

In the original edition, Helen writes heart-wrenchingly about her fears over infant mortality and future tragedies that may befall her child: '[...] one of two thoughts is ever at hand to check my swelling bliss; the one: "He may be taken from me;" the other: "He may live to curse his own existence."'[13] The rest of the chapter details Arthur's almost complete indifference to his son; he is quite happy to ignore him, only noticing baby Arthur when he feels like gloating, or when Helen's affections towards the baby incite ridiculous feelings of jealousy in him:

> At present, he is pleased with the acquisition, and that is nearly all I can say. At first, it was a thing to wonder and laugh at, not to touch: now, it is an object almost of indifference, except when his impatience is roused by its "utter helplessness" and "imperturbable stupidity" (as he calls it), or my too close attention to its wants.[14]

The next scene sees Arthur protesting when Helen hands the baby to him in the hopes that more interaction between the two will help them to bond. Of course, Arthur betrays his selfish nature once again by refusing to love the child until it is older and can show affection itself. In the 1854 edition, all of Helen's fears and Arthur's dialogue have been cut, leaving only Helen's joy at becoming a mother. Anne's pointed criticism of fathers who don't take part in their children's lives is missing.

As Samantha Ellis writes, 'Anne is calling on men to take responsibility for their children, to enjoy being fathers, to recognise how hard and wonderful motherhood is and the value and share it. Cutting all this, and leaving just her gratitude, makes her sound like a pious, blissed-out yummy mummy.'[15]

It's easy to understand Ellis's fury, especially when you consider that she admits to being someone who had been led to believe that Anne was 'a bit, well, boring'.[16] It seems that Ellis feels cheated out of discovering an author she could have been enjoying earlier, all because of a set of circumstances that were out of Anne's control. There is a sense of injustice on Anne's behalf – if only she had been alive to authorise a new edition, or Charlotte had let her own publisher, Smith, Elder & Co, bring out their own edition of it first. Anne may still have been compared unfavourably to her sisters, but at least renewed interest in her works wouldn't have been slowed by the existence of an inferior edition.

The 1854 *Parlour Library* edition became the standard edition of the text for about the next 130 years. When Smith, Elder & Co released the 1857–60 edition of the *Brontë Life and Works*, it featured a version of *Wildfell Hall* based on the *Parlour Library* text. When G.D. Hargreaves was writing about the text in 1977, he found only three editions of *Wildfell Hall* (not including the Newby editions) that included the full text: the Nelson edition (1905), the Gresham Publishing Co edition (1905) and the *Shakespeare Head Brontë* edition (1931). Of those, only the Nelson edition was still in print. The *Shakespeare Head Brontë* is still considered as one of the best editions of the Brontës' works and of Elizabeth Gaskell's *Life Of Charlotte Brontë*, and the books in that edition are highly sought-after collector's items.[17]

Thankfully, I now find it is more likely – if you go to a

bookshop, rather than buy online – that you're going to pick up a copy of the original text based on the first Newby edition, and which will also contain Anne's important preface to the second edition. The most recent Oxford University Press, Vintage and Everyman's Library editions contain the full text with the preface. Most of the more ornate editions that you can find in 'beautiful books' sections of bookshops will have the complete text, though there are a couple of exceptions (they are deceptively pretty, and it's all the more disappointing that the kind of care that has gone into the design has not gone into the text). Stevie Davies' 1996 edition, published by Penguin Classics, is my preferred edition – Davies clearly loves her subject, and her introduction and notes are incredibly thorough, contextualising Anne and her writing in such a way as to enrich the experience of reading the novel.

The best way to make sure you're buying an edition containing the full, unabridged text is to check the beginning of the book for Anne's preface and also for Gilbert's letter to J. Halford. If you pick up a copy that begins with 'You must go back with me to the autumn of 1827', you are reading an incomplete text. If there is a 'Preface to the Second Edition', followed by a letter beginning 'To J. Halford, Esq.' then you probably have a complete text.

Elizabeth Gaskell.

Buying online is a different matter, as it's not always clear or easy to discover which edition they are selling. My incomplete copy of the text came from a 'print to order' service, selling through an online retailer, and which claims to be an 'unabridged edition based on the first edition.' If possible, try to check any sample pages that the seller will let you look at. If you download a free version, you can make the same checks as you would with a physical book. Otherwise, you can look at some of the sample pages to see if there are chapter headings. If chapter headings are present as well as chapter numbers, then you probably have a copy of the complete text. If there are no chapter headings, just numbers, it is likely that you have an edition based on the heavily edited text.

Since learning about the treatment of Anne's works, I've wondered how many other authors have been edited in similar ways. I urge anyone interested in Anne to find copies of both the complete and incomplete texts, just so that you can experience for yourself the impact of the huge changes that were made. It's one thing to read about them, it's another thing entirely to read the truncated version of Anne's text and watch the pious, less imaginative, and less powerful version of Anne begin to materialise.

EDITING ANNE'S POETRY

Not long after the deaths of her sisters, Charlotte's publisher asked her if they could republish Emily and Anne's novels. They also asked if there was any other unpublished material that she was willing to let them include in new editions. She initially agreed to the republication of *Wuthering Heights* and *Agnes Grey*, and refused to include any previously unpublished poetry, But she quickly changed her mind and, in the end, selected and edited a collection of Anne and Emily's poetry for inclusion in an 1850 edition of *Wuthering Heights* and *Agnes Grey*.[18] The edits that Charlotte made to Anne and Emily's poetry were substantial. Some of the changes were simple spelling and grammar corrections, and some were necessary in order to remove references to Gondal.[19] All three of the sisters had edited their poems together in the same way for the verses that appeared in *Poems* in 1846, removing all traces of their imaginary worlds, so these changes were not too intrusive.

But the other changes that Charlotte made to Anne and Emily's poetry are harder to understand. Eight of Anne's poems were chosen along with seventeen of Emily's, and Charlotte's edits were so drastic in some places that she completely removed stanzas and replaced Anne and Emily's original lines with lines of her own. Juliet Barker writes that, in the case of four of Emily's poems, 'Charlotte actually added between four and eight lines of her own composition, usually to bring the poem to an end.'[20] (Claire O'Callaghan wrote more about the effect of Charlotte's editing on Emily's poetry in *Emily Brontë Reappraised*.[21])

When it came to choosing and editing Anne's poetry, there's a sense that Charlotte picked poems that fit the narrative she had built up around her youngest sister. She chose not to include poems that were similar in subjects and themes to the poems she chose of Emily's, possibly because she viewed Anne as the inferior poet. Both Emily and Anne wrote poems called 'The Bluebell' that frame bluebells as sad reminders of home, and happier summer days. Only Emily's bluebell poem was chosen for the 1850 edition.

Anne's poem 'To —' didn't make the cut either. As we saw in Chapter Two, this poem is often seen as being romantic in tone, and it's possible that Charlotte didn't include it because of a desire to protect Anne. Edward Chitham suggests that

'To —', along with another of Anne's poems called 'Night', was effectively 'suppressed': 'the literary quality of both poems is relatively good. The content of both, however, is revealing and might very well be thought by Charlotte to imply some betrayal of Anne's maidenly modesty.'[22]

The subject of 'Night' is a romantic interest who has passed away. The narrator appears to be wishing away the daylight hours in order to be able to see their loved one in their dreams:

> I love the silent hour of night,
> For blissful dreams may then arise,
> Revealing to my charmèd sight
> What may not bless my waking eyes!
>
> And then a voice may meet my ear
> That death had silenced long ago;
> And hope and rapture may appear
> Instead of solitude and woe.
>
> Cold in the grave for years has lain
> The form it was my bliss to see,
> And only dreams can bring again
> The darling of my heart to me.[23]

The poem is simple, and its simplicity makes the final lines all the more powerful. There is no hope of the narrator ever seeing the darling of their heart again. It's vulnerable in a way that is typical of Anne's 'pillar of witness' style of poems; it is straightforward and honest in its portrayal of the narrator's feelings. In this case, the desolate sadness at the thought that only sleep can bring back the comfort of their loved one.

It's curious that Charlotte would choose to exclude these

romantic poems and yet include Emily's 'Last Words', a scathing backlash of the narrator against an unfaithful lover:

I can forget black eyes and brows,
And lips of rosy charm,
If you forget the sacred vows
Those faithless lips could form.[24]

If Charlotte left out Anne's 'To —' and 'Night' because she wanted to protect Anne's modesty, she clearly didn't employ the same tactic with Emily.

The poems that Charlotte chose to include all emphasised Anne's religious melancholy, her burdened heart, and a generally bleak outlook on life. She renamed 'Monday Night' as 'Domestic Bliss': it is a poem about a feeling of unrest where there should be none in a seemingly happy domestic scene. 'Despondency', 'Confidence' and 'The Narrow Way' all follow the theme of calling on God, the narrator's redeemer, to help them avoid falling into a life of sin. But Charlotte managed to tone them down, even while presenting poems that fit the image of Anne she was trying to present. The last lines of 'Despondency' originally read 'Lord Jesus, save me lest I die, / And hear a wretch's prayer.'[25] In Charlotte's edit, the word 'wretch' is removed, and the last line replaced by 'Christ, hear my humble prayer!', a much less powerful alternative. In using the word 'wretch', Anne's depth of feeling takes her humility to the extreme. 'Christ, hear my humble prayer!' simply falls flat in comparison.

Charlotte made other edits like this, going so far as to insert her own lines and remove stanzas according to her stylistic choices. Most of the lines she re-wrote or removed resulted in sections that felt clunky and jarring, giving the impression that Anne was indeed a less experienced writer than Emily, lacking her originality and power. And Charlotte's influence has had long-lasting consequences: a Google search for Anne's poetry will result in confusing and incomplete lists, some of which contain duplicates of poems without making it clear which ones are the versions edited by Charlotte. Unless you already know exactly what you're looking for, it's very hard to find online versions of the poems that are based on Anne's original manuscripts.

The poem that received the largest number of edits and the most infuriating changes was Anne's last, published in the 1850 edition of *Wuthering Heights* and *Agnes Grey* as 'Last Lines'. It was edited and named by Charlotte but before discussing her changes, it is worth first experiencing Anne's original poem in full:

A dreadful darkness closes in
　　On my bewildered mind;
O let me suffer and not sin,
　　Be tortured yet resigned.

Through all this world of whelming mist
　　Still let me look to Thee,
And give me courage to resist
　　The Tempter till he flee.

Weary I am — O give me strength
　　And leave me not to faint;
Say Thou wilt comfort me at length
　　And pity my complaint.

I've begged to serve Thee heart and soul,
　　To sacrifice to Thee
No niggard portion, but the whole
　　Of my identity.

I hoped amid the brave and strong
    My portioned task might lie,
To toil amid the labouring throng
    With purpose pure and high.

But Thou hast fixed another part,
    And Thou hast fixed it well;
I said so with my breaking heart
    When first the anguish fell.

For Thou hast taken my delight
    And hope of life away,
And bid me watch the painful night
    And wait the weary day.

The hope and the delight were Thine;
    I bless Thee for their loan;
I gave Thee while I deemed them mine
    Too little thanks, I own.

Shall I with joy Thy blessings share
    And not endure their loss?
Or hope the martyr's crown to wear
    And cast away the cross?

These weary hours will not be lost,
    These days of passive misery,
These nights of darkness anguish lost
    If I can fix my heart on Thee.

The wretch that weak and weary lies
    Crushed with sorrow, worn with pain,

Still to heaven may lift his eyes
And strive and labour not in vain;

Weak and weary though I lie,
Crushed with sorrow, worn with pain,
Still I may lift to Heaven mine eyes
And strive and labour not in vain,

That inward strife against the sins
That ever wait on suffering;
To watch and strike where first begins
Each ill that would corruption bring,

That secret labour to sustain
With humble patience every blow,
To gather fortitude from pain
And hope and holiness from woe.

Thus let me serve Thee from my heart
Whatever be my written fate,
Whether thus early to depart
Or yet awhile to wait.

If Thou should bring me back to life
More humbled should I be;
More wise, more strengthened for the strife,
More apt to lean on Thee.

Should Death be standing at the gate
Thus should I keep my vow;
But, Lord, whate'er my future fate
So let me serve Thee now.[26]

Anne began writing this poem in January 1849, two days after she had been diagnosed with tuberculosis. The physician was able only to offer treatments that would prolong Anne's life and reduce the pain, not a cure.[27]

The poem can be split into two parts; Anne wrote the first nine stanzas in pencil, starting on 7 January, and completed the rest of the poem in ink, writing 'finished 28th Jan' at the bottom. The first nine stanzas of the poem were written with the immediate despair that Anne must have been experiencing after her diagnosis. They read as a record of anguish as the narrator realises that their future plans are about to be cut short. She can no longer count herself among those who strive to take advantage of the lives given to them, who try to do some good in the world, and that breaks her heart. It's a very different message to that which we are used to associating with Anne – there's no desire to be in heaven, there's no resignation to death. Instead there's an internal struggle and strong emotions of fear, panic and a sense that this is unfair. This is not what the author, what Anne, wants.

The second half of the poem, concluded a few weeks later, followed a brief reprieve in Anne's illness. She wasn't much better, but she didn't appear to be getting worse. Charlotte wrote to Ellen that Anne's coughs had seemed to become less frequent. Anne was very outwardly calm too, trying not to give in to despair, and the second half of the poem seems to reflect this. Anne writes about how even if she can't live a longer life serving God and honouring her beliefs, at least she can stay true to those ideals while she is alive. She even goes so far as to hope that she might recover.

The poem ends, if not hopefully, then at least more positively than it began. The whole poem reads almost as a conversation with the self, an attempt to reconcile the knowledge of the narrator's own mortality with retaining a sense of dignity and purpose. Anne spends four stanzas almost bitterly reflecting the fact that she has given the whole of her identity to her faith, and so God's decision to end her life so soon feels almost like a betrayal – if Anne had written a purely angry poem, I don't think there's anyone who could blame her for expressing her feelings in such a way.

But, of course, Anne doesn't do this. To give in to sadness, to any anger she may have had, would have been to give in to sin. To betray herself in spite of her faith and in front of her God would have been worse than to be betrayed by him. Instead, Anne reasons with herself, employing the thoughtfulness and patience that she applied to her everyday life. In the poem she acknowledges that, in accordance with her faith, the hope and delight of life were never truly hers to begin with and expresses gratitude for the loan of both. The poem begins with a dreadful darkness and a bewildered mind, the panic and claustrophobia of someone who has just received a death sentence. Anne's poem works through that despair and confusion, landing on a much more controlled final stanza. The narrator has made a conscious decision about how she will approach her situation. She wants to live, but if God decides otherwise, she will meet her fate with dignity. All while staying true to her beliefs.

Charlotte chose only eight of the original seventeen stanzas to publish in the 1850 edition of *Wuthering Heights* and *Agnes Grey*. The first four stanzas, the ones expressing Anne's despair and religious doubt, were removed. Instead, Charlotte chose to begin the poem with 'I hoped that with the brave and strong…' and avoids any mention of the weakness of the narrator in the face of death. The regret at the loss of future life is reduced to one stanza, which is then followed by a resigned acceptance and the hope that the narrator can serve God while still alive.

Edward Chitham's editorial notes on 'Last Lines' do not acknowledge Charlotte's edit of the poem, other than to say that he won't include her alterations. It is a stance that puts me in mind of Stevie Davies' dismissal of the 1854 text of *Wildfell Hall* as 'worthless' (see Chapter Two). I am including Charlotte's version here in full, to make it easier to see just how substantial her changes were:

I hoped that with the brave and strong
My portioned task might lie;
To toil amid the busy throng,
With purpose pure and high.

But God has fixed another part,
And he has fixed it well:
I said so with my bleeding heart,
When first the anguish fell.

Thou God, hast taken our delight,
Our treasured hope, away;
Thou bid'st us now weep through the night,
And sorrow through the day.

These weary hours will not be lost,
These days of misery,—
These nights of darkness, anguish-tost,—
Can I but turn to Thee.

With secret labour to sustain
In humble patience every blow;
To gather fortitude from pain,

And hope and holiness from woe.

Thus let me serve Thee from my heart,
Whate'er may be my written fate;
Whether thus early to depart,
Or yet a while to wait.

If Thou shouldest bring me back to life,
More humbled I should be;
More wise—more strengthened for the strife,
More apt to lean on Thee.

Should death be standing at the gate,
Thus should I keep my vow;
But, Lord, whatever be my fate,
Oh let me serve Thee now![28]

The last line feels much more dramatic in Charlotte's version, while somehow feeling emptier than Anne's much humbler 'So let me serve Thee now'. Charlotte's dramatic ending implies blind faith, and an eagerness to serve, even if that involves dying. Anne's ending is much more decisive and final; it carries the weight of knowledge of her own death and, as such, has a greater impact on the reader.

Charlotte also completely changed the meaning and impact of the verse 'For Thou hast taken my delight / And hope of life away', changing the verse itself to 'Thou God, hast taken our delight, / Our treasured hope, away; / Thou bid'st us now weep through the night, / And sorrow through the day.' Juliet Barker has suggested that Charlotte changed this verse to make it about the death of Emily, rather than Anne's sadness over having her own hopes for a long and purposeful life taken away. She argues that Charlotte's changes are 'therefore not only a clumsier alternative but also a misinterpretation of the original'.[29] 'Clumsy' is a good word to describe most of the edits that Charlotte made to both Anne and Emily's poetry. She even changed 'I said so with my breaking heart' to 'I said so with my bleeding heart', softening the sentiment behind the line and robbing it of its original power.

Like with *Wildfell Hall*, the altered version of Anne's last poem became the more popular and more readily available version. Recent collections of Brontë poetry have fixed this, but Edward Chitham's *The Poems of Anne Brontë* is now out of print. Chitham's book is a comprehensive and very thorough collection of Anne's poems, containing an autobiographical section and extensive notes on each poem. It builds on the work done by Charles W. Hatfield and Clement Shorter, who published a collection of Anne's poems in 1920. Hatfield also worked on correctly assigning poems to Anne that had mistakenly been attributed to Emily (some of Emily's poems had also been attributed to Anne). Juliet Barker edited a selection of Brontë poems for Everyman's Library, which came out in 1993. It contains a selection of some of Anne's best poems, again with extensive and informative notes, but it is not a complete collection.

The Brontës: Tales of Glass Town, Angria and Gondal contains twenty of Anne's Gondal poems. These include three of the poems that can be found in the 1846 *Poems*, again with extensive notes for all of the poems, including information about manuscripts and the changes that were made when the poems were published.

There are lots of editions of Anne's poetry available to buy online, but there's no guarantee that the poems inside are based on Anne's originals rather than Charlotte's edits. Neither is it possible to find out if they are complete collections, or if they advertise themselves as 'complete and unabridged' in the same way that print-to-order incomplete editions of *Wildfell Hall* claim to be. Copies of the 1846 *Poems* are readily available and since they tend to be based on the first edition it can be assumed that the poems appear as all three of the sisters intended them to.

There are plenty of poetry websites that publish Anne's poetry online, including some that are entirely dedicated to the poems of the Brontës and even Anne on her own. It's very difficult to know if you're reading versions based on Anne's original manuscripts, however, much in the same way that it's difficult to know which version of *Wildfell Hall* you are reading unless you know what to look for. Anne's last poem exists online in a few different versions. It is possible to find her original version, and that appears almost as often as Charlotte's version does. More common than either is a mash-up of the two; there are versions that take Charlotte's version and add a few more of the original verses to the poem.

AN IMAGINARY ANNE

The author of *Wildfell Hall* and *Agnes Grey* holds strong opinions, expresses her ideas and personal philosophies eloquently (without detracting from the narrative), and writes in a deceptively simple style that reflects the author's deep commitment to getting her point across while creating an entertaining story. The Anne that often appears in popular culture, however, is shy, retiring, overly religious and moralising, and generally considered to be less talented than her sisters. She is dear, gentle Anne, delicate since birth. Anyone coming to *Wildfell Hall* for the first time, with this incomplete and often untrue picture of Anne as their only context, will be presented with the question: how do you reconcile the image of the author of *Wildfell Hall* with the portrait of Anne Brontë that has survived in the popular imagination?

As we've just seen, some of Anne's works were changed so drastically that meanings were lost and the edited versions were open to further misinterpretation. Her skill and subtlety was also often lost, giving rise to the opinion that Anne lacked the talent, originality and imagination of her sisters. But what about the idea that Anne was fragile – feeble even? 'Meek' and 'mild' are words often associated with Anne, too, and a lot of these descriptors of her personality have their source in Charlotte's 'Biographical Notice'. They were emphasised by Ellen Nussey's *Reminiscences* and solidified in Elizabeth Gaskell's *The Life of Charlotte Brontë*.

Anyone who has lost a close friend or relative can appreciate how painful it is to sort through the belongings they leave behind, and Charlotte suffered three such losses in a very short period of time. Her sisters had been lifelong collaborators, from their time spent creating and writing about sprawling imaginary worlds, to making plans to start a school, to finally writing and publishing their poems and novels together. Even through her grief (or perhaps because of it), Charlotte felt that her sisters' lasting reputations should not focus on the coarseness and vulgarity they had been accused of by reviewers and critics. In her 'Biographical Notice', Charlotte wrote that she 'felt it a sacred duty to wipe the dust off their gravestones, and leave their dear names free from soil'.[30]

When reading about the choices Charlotte made concerning Anne's work, it's easy to paint Charlotte as a terrible sister, as someone out to portray Anne as the inferior to herself and Emily. As we've already seen, there is plenty of evidence to suggest that Charlotte saw Anne as the baby of the family and treated her as such. Charlotte comes across as a slightly patronising older sister who completely misunderstands the point of Anne's work (like with *Wildfell Hall*). As such, Charlotte is often credited with destroying her youngest sister's reputation and literary legacy. But I don't want to fall into the trap of presenting 'Charlotte-as-bitch', a movement that Lucasta Miller describes in her book *The Brontë Myth*.[31]

People have spent a long time looking for skeletons in Charlotte's closet, and psychobiographers tried to find explanations for her writing and personality.

Biographers and critics have compared Charlotte's negative traits (her desire to be in control, her hard-heartedness, self-denial and neurotic tendencies) with Emily's much more desirable traits. Over the years, Emily started to emerge as the mysterious woman of the moors, and even Branwell has been portrayed as having been failed by his oldest sister. The facts of their lives took on different meanings depending on who was doing the interpreting, and Charlotte almost always seemed to come out looking the worst. The Brontës inspire such strong emotions in those who are interested in them, that it sometimes seems like people forget that they were all real individuals, with complex inner lives, rather than the two-dimensional caricatures they have often been reduced to.

Samantha Ellis's book *Take Courage* is one of the best Brontë biographies, and yet it still comes close to falling into the Charlotte-hating trap. While it is true that Charlotte and Anne were not close during their time together at Roe Head, it is unfair to reduce Charlotte's motivations for this emotional separation to selfishness and meanness. A passage on Charlotte's self-hatred, as expressed to Ellen Nussey, is followed in Samantha Ellis's book by the line 'She didn't even notice when Anne fell ill.' Juliet Barker, Winifred Gérin and Samantha

Ellis all write about Charlotte's argument with Miss Wooler, during which she accused the headmistress of neglecting her younger sister's health. They also write about Charlotte's own apparent neglect of Anne at this time, but where Barker and Gérin give sympathy to Charlotte and her situation, Samantha Ellis accuses Charlotte of lashing out at Miss Wooler, 'accusing her of what she felt guilty of herself: neglecting Anne'.[32]

One of the things that always comes up when talking to people about the Brontës is which member of the family is your favourite, or which book, or even which poem. It's a fun way to get really nerdy about some of your best-loved books with people who are similarly nerdy, but a trend I don't enjoy is to pit the sisters against each other. Their relationships with each other will always be a source of fascination and can even give us better insight into their writing, but in order to look at these things objectively it's sometimes necessary to take an emotional step back. As attached as we might get, as much as we would like to think that we know and understand them, there's no way of definitively knowing the intricate details of their sibling relationships. We misinterpret and misunderstand people in our own lives on a daily basis, sometimes by accident, sometimes because of bias we may or may not be aware of. It's important to remember this when reading any kind of biography, not just those about the Brontës, and keep in mind that it's very difficult to see them through a lens unclouded by the myths that have been built up around them.

Bearing all that in mind, it is nonetheless undeniable that the Anne presented by Charlotte in her 'Biographical Notice' stuck around for a very long time. In making her sisters appear reclusive, and ignorant of the world around them, Charlotte may have thought that she was excusing their writing in the sense that they didn't know any better:

> Neither Emily or Anne was learned; they had no thought of filling their pitchers at the well-spring of other minds; they always wrote from the impulse of nature, the dictates of intuition, and from such stores of observation as their limited experience had enabled them to amass.[33]

Charlotte must have been aware of the lies she was telling in writing this 'Biographical Notice' – both Emily and Anne had attended schools during their lifetime. All the Brontë children had enthusiastically approached their studies from a young age. But an ignorant, sheltered and gentle woman is much easier to forgive than one who writes vulgar novels and knows exactly what she is doing.

The Anne in Charlotte's 'Biographical Notice' is firmly in Emily's shadow:

> Anne's character was milder and more subdued; she wanted the power, the fire, the originality of her sister, but was well-endowed with quiet virtues of her own. Long-suffering, self-denying, reflective, and intelligent, a constitutional reserve and taciturnity placed and kept her in the shade, and covered her mind, and especially her feelings, with a sort of nun-like veil, which was rarely lifted.'[34]

There are definitely positive statements here – 'intelligent', 'reflective' – but these things tend to be overlooked when you compare them to the other not-quite compliments. At the time Charlotte was writing this, self-denial was a kind of religious virtue (though now it might be seen as a form of masochism) and there is also nothing wrong with possessing 'quiet' virtues. But what turns this praise into not-quite compliments is the stark contrast it makes with the descriptions of Emily. Emily has the romantic, free-spirited nature associated with genius. To call Anne quiet after such a description of her sister, as well as saying that she wanted the power of Emily, comes across as somewhat sinister. Emily didn't care what people thought, but Anne was quiet and reserved, just like a woman of the time should be.

Mrs Gaskell's Anne is just as Charlotte described in her 'Biographical Notice'. She barely registers as a person, until her final illness, when around ten pages are dedicated to Anne's poor health, Charlotte's worry for her youngest sister, and a detailed account of Anne's final days. Mrs Gaskell included Charlotte's edited version of Anne's last poem too, cementing her representation as someone who wished for death.

Charlotte echoed this sentiment in two letters that she wrote to her publisher, William Smith Williams, shortly after Anne's death. It is unfortunate that the image that has stuck from these two letters is of a woman fated to suffer an 'early death', who saw life as a 'burden' and longed 'to be gone'. Charlotte's grief and pain radiate from the pages, and I have always thought that maybe part of Charlotte's insistence that Anne was destined for an early grave was a way to console herself. If Anne's early death was inevitable, it might be easier for Charlotte to take. But she writes to Williams 'it but half consoles to remember this calm – there is piercing pain in it'.[35]

Ellen Nussey told a slightly different story. Her appraisal of Anne and her characteristics always comes across as much more measured, though she still infantilises Anne somewhat. Ellen gives us our only physical description of Anne in her *Reminiscences*:

> Anne – dear, gentle Anne – was quite different in appearance from the others. She was her aunt's favourite. Her

> hair was a very pretty, light brown, and fell on her neck in graceful curls. She had lovely violet-blue eyes, fine pencilled eyebrows, and clear, almost transparent complexion.[36]

We also have three portraits of Anne drawn by Charlotte, with a potential fourth. All of Charlotte's portraits of Anne fit with Ellen's physical description – she is drawn with fine features and delicate curls. Charlotte clearly admired her sister and drew her as an attractive young woman, particularly in her portrait dated 17 April 1833. Anne is in profile, in romantic pose and dress that would not have been out of place on an Angrian or Gondolian heroine.

Charlotte also admired Anne's 'extraordinary heroism of endurance' in the face of the distress she suffered as a result of asthma.[37] And Charlotte did describe Anne's poems as having 'the merit of truth and simplicity'.[38] She wrote of how walks on the moors reminded her of Anne: 'The distant prospects were Anne's delight, and when I look round, she is in the blue tints, the pale mists, the waves and shadows of the horizon.'[39]

Even though we can find praise of Anne in Charlotte's correspondence and in some of the positive reviews of Anne's work, it is the negative and dramatic descriptions of Anne that have endured. Elizabeth Gaskell used Anne as a prop to exaggerate Charlotte's role as the selfless elder sister, who made huge sacrifices to care for her family, especially the frail and delicate youngest sister. This, combined with the posthumous editing of Anne's work almost beyond recognition, pushed Anne into obscurity. As Lucasta Miller says in *The Brontë Myth*, 'for most of her posthumous life she was regarded as very much the least interesting sister, mentioned, it seems, merely to make up the number three'.[40]

A portrait by Charlotte of thirteen-year-old Anne.

I have a lot of friends who love Charlotte and Emily but don't necessarily know very much about Anne. One of these friends, who is a particular fan of *Wuthering Heights*, once played the part of Arthur Bell Nicholls in Polly Teale's play *Brontë*. I asked him what he remembered of Anne's character in the play. His response: 'Poor sweet Anne was a bit of a wet wally. Such is her lot in life!' Portrayals of Anne have not always been very kind; the narrative of the weak-from-birth, timid and retiring younger sister is one that most people have become comfortable with, and so it gets perpetuated.

I take particular offence at Muriel Spark's statement that Anne 'could "pen" a story well enough' and was the 'literary equivalent of a decent water-colourist', which is dismissive and incredibly insulting.[41] It implies that Anne treated her work as an 'accomplishment', something to achieve only to make oneself more attractive. It suggests that her writing was without direction, something done merely to pass the time or to make herself look good.

Anne is so well known for being an unknown that she even made it into an episode of *Family Guy*. Stewie says to his sister Meg, 'You're not the first person to be outshined by a sibling. What about the third Brontë sister?' The scene then cuts to Charlotte and Emily, sitting in the parsonage, drinking tea and complimenting each other on their success (they both speak in a wildly inaccurate accent – Received Pronunciation). They are suddenly interrupted by Anne, who crudely (in a bad Cockney accent) shouts, 'I made blood out me lady parts!' Charlotte and Emily praise her as they would a small child: 'Good for you, so we've all done something!'

There even exist biographies of the Brontës that almost completely gloss over Anne altogether. *The Brontës: Charlotte and Emily*, written by Laura Hinkley and published in the 1940s, doesn't even acknowledge Anne in the title. All of Charlotte and Emily's books get their own chapter, even *The Professor*, Charlotte's least well known first novel that wasn't published until after her death. The biographical chapter on Anne begins, 'The youngest, prettiest, gentlest, least gifted, and physically frailest of the Brontës emerged into womanhood under the sheltering care of her sisters.'[42] That first line sums up very well the typical attitudes towards Anne until they began to change in the 1960s.

A SHIFTING REPUTATION

Kate Beaton's comic strip *Dude Watchin' With The Brontës* is one of the funniest depictions of the Brontës in popular culture. Charlotte and Emily are seen swooning over unpleasant, drunken 'hunks', one of whom rudely asks, 'What the hell are you looking at?' Anne quite rightly observes, 'That guy was an asshole!', which prompts Charlotte to say, 'Honestly Anne you have *no* taste.' Charlotte and Emily continue to ogle passing drunkards, calling them brooding and handsome, to which Anne says, 'If you like alcoholic dickbags!' Emily and Charlotte are outraged: 'Anne you are *so* inappropriate!' 'No wonder nobody buys *your* books'.

Emily and Charlotte's problematic, crude leading male characters have, over time, inexplicably become romantic heroes. *Wildfell Hall*, which was more shocking than any of the other Bell books at the time, slowly morphed into a religious morality tale, devoid of 'brooding hunks'. Rosalie Murray in *Agnes Grey* naïvely observes that 'reformed rakes make the best husbands, *everybody* knows.'[43] Anne's mistake in writing *Wildfell Hall* was turning Arthur Huntingdon into a drunken abuser, when clearly she should have turned him into a reformed rake like *Jane Eyre's* Mr Rochester (hopefully my sarcasm here is apparent!). The great joke in *Dude Watchin' With The Brontës* is that Kate Beaton is well aware that Anne's realistic approach was aimed at warning people away from such characters – she refused to romanticise characters such as Heathcliff and Mr Rochester.

If popular attitudes towards the Brontës have changed so much, how have critical opinions? Winifred Gérin's biography of Anne, published in 1959, was the first sympathetic biography that was entirely dedicated to the youngest Brontë. While it's true that she relied too much on interpreting Anne's works as autobiographical, she set a new precedent for re-imagining Anne and her life and character. Anne is no longer in the shadow of her sisters, in Gérin's opinion; by scratching ever so slightly beneath the surface, she began to uncover a much more interesting Anne. Underneath Anne's 'nun-like veil', Gérin discovered that there existed a brave, thoughtful and serious young woman. Charlotte, and Mrs Gaskell, said that the choice of subject when it came to *Wildfell Hall* was a mistake, and 'was painfully discordant to one who would fain have sheltered herself from all but peaceful and religious ideas'.[44] Gérin, on the other hand, said of the creation of *Wildfell Hall*:

> With the legal position of women still supporting the immoral favouritism accorded men, Anne was not likely to engage the sympathy of her hearers unless she used strong measures. Strong measures alone would do. By the very nature of the task she set herself she was bound to

> be uncompromising. She had to present at first hand, not in reported narration, a series of scenes exhibiting men and women at their most bestial, else the revulsion she needed to create would be too adulterated to take effect.
>
> Very rightly, since such was her objective, Anne renders her debauchees both repulsive and alarming, but, if that was a fault, she committed a fault also in making them hideously menacing and alive.[45]

In 1979, Edward Chitham published a complete collection of Anne's poems, with commentaries that asserted Anne's place as a very logical and analytical thinker. Poems like 'Self-Communion' and 'The Three Guides' demonstrate Anne's ability to express her complex and self-reflective nature (see Chapter Two). They do have a 'sweet sincere pathos', as Charlotte said in her 'Biographical Notice', but that doesn't automatically mean that their quality is low. Far from it – Chitham notes how her more personal poems have 'transparency and sincerity. Anne seems to be striving for an austere style, working to communicate as directly as possible and in a totally uncoloured way, without rhetoric or artificiality.'[46] His biography of Anne in 1991 built on Winifred Gérin's biography, presenting Anne in a sympathetic light. The biggest difference was that he was a lot more careful when it came to analysing Anne's work in an autobiographical context.

Interest in Anne Brontë's works increased in the 1960s and '70s, when feminist criticism of literature was on the rise. Anne's social commentary, particularly in relation to women, was of particular interest (see Chapter Six for her writing about the roles that women were expected to play, the options that were open to them, and what a woman could expect from marriage).

As a result, new editions of *Agnes Grey* and *Wildfell Hall* became much more widely available than they used to be. *Wildfell Hall* is probably the most popular, but even *Agnes Grey*, the book that was mostly ignored by contemporary critics, has seen a revival. I've managed to make a few of my friends read it, and all were surprised by just how readable it was. One friend is convinced that Anne was the voice of her generation – a hidden generation of educated, middle-class women whose only options were to get married or go into servitude.

In her introduction to the 1988 Penguin Classics edition, Angeline Goreau says, 'For modern readers, *Agnes Grey* serves as an important historical document. There is perhaps no other novel of the period which gives such an intimately revealing account of the quotidian horrors of the only "respectable" employment open to a gentlewoman in the mid-nineteenth century – that of governess.' While *Jane Eyre* also presents the life of a governess, Jane herself finds that she can converse with her employer almost as an equal; she eventually marries him and is removed from her life of drudgery. Agnes's life is firmly rooted in realism and is much more brutal for it. Her loneliness and suppression of self strike a chord with anyone who has had to pretend to be something other than themselves to be accepted in a workplace. Anne does admittedly make Agnes marry, but she is not saved from drudgery, she is not elevated by her marriage. Agnes marries a clergyman, fully aware that her life will always include the work of a clergyman's wife.

In 2016, *Guardian* journalist Lucy Mangan appeared in the BBC programme *Being the Brontës* and declared that *Agnes Grey* was her favourite Brontë novel. This was certainly the first time I had ever experienced anyone saying that Anne was the Brontë sister who spoke to them most. She presented Anne's novel as groundbreaking in its portrayal of the life of a governess. 2016 also saw a new biography by Nick Holland, and then in 2017 Samantha Ellis wrote *Take Courage: Anne Brontë and the Art of Life*, in which she wrote about discovering that Anne was not the 'boring Brontë' that she had always been led to believe that she was.

The most recent Brontë biopic, Sally Wainwright's BBC drama *To Walk Invisible*, has a wonderful portrayal of Anne. Outwardly she appears timid, often nervous, particularly during Charlotte and Anne's trip to London to visit Charlotte's publisher. But it isn't presented as a passive shyness; Charlie Murphy plays an Anne who is present, who pays attention, and who cares deeply about the people around her. She is seen with her sisters on the moors, her ill health barely alluded to. And the only time she breaks down is after Branwell's dismissal from Thorp Green. She doesn't cry for herself, but for her brother and how she could have done more to help him. When I imagine Anne Brontë, that's who I see: an observant and perceptive woman striving to do some good in the world. She continually tried to be a better person so that she could better help others.

FOUR

ANNE IN NATURE

It's well known that all the Brontë children loved the moors that surround Haworth. They had been avid walkers and lovers of nature since early childhood, and such easy access to the moors from the back garden of the parsonage offered plenty of encouragement for indulging in both. As part of the Brontë bicentenary celebrations, four stones engraved with new poems inspired by the family were placed in significant locations in the landscape between Haworth and Thornton (the parsonage and the Brontë birthplace). Walks were devised that take in the stones and some of the moorland that the Brontës loved so much, including a hike across the Brontë Bridge and up to Top Withins, one of the supposed inspirations for *Wuthering Heights.*

Elizabeth Gaskell's *The Life of Charlotte Brontë* offered a very biased view of the lives of the Brontës and of Haworth and its surrounding areas. Even the moors didn't escape Mrs Gaskell's attempts to make the reader sympathise towards Charlotte and the hard life that she had led:

> All round the horizon there is this same line of sinuous wave-like hills; the scoops into which they fall only revealing other hills beyond, of similar colour and shape, crowned with wild, bleak moors—grand, from the ideas of solitude and loneliness which they suggest, or oppressive from the feeling which they give of being pent-up by some monotonous and illimitable barrier, according to the mood of mind in which the spectator may be.[1]

Anyone who has been to Haworth or walked across the moors knows that Mrs Gaskell's description is not completely true. They are grand, but they are far from bleak. Even in the winter, if you go out on a clear day the moors seem bright and alive. Winifred Gérin's description of the moors is much more accurate. For her, the moors are 'perpetually clothed in splendour' and 'there is a nobility in this stretch of country that is an enemy to petty thoughts; the whole scene is nothing less than elevating'.[2]

It is unsurprising then that the moors played a central role in the lives of all the Brontës, who enjoyed being so close to nature. A favourite book among the children was Bewick's *A History of British Birds*, and the circulating library at Keighley was sure to hold books on natural history. The Brontës grew up in a time that has since been called 'the heyday of natural history': enthusiasts collected butterflies, birds' eggs, insects and anything they could examine. And the poets of the time, also, were heavily influenced by the natural world – Wordsworth, Southey and Coleridge were particularly beloved by the Brontës.

From the subtle language of flowers, to the increasing concern for animal welfare, the natural world was a huge influence on Anne's work too.

Bewick's portrait of a heron, in A History of British Birds.

RESPITE IN NATURE

Anne used her ability to write vividly and emotionally about nature to create idyllic spaces within her poems and novels. Often, these idyllic scenes are in direct contrast to the circumstances of the protagonist, causing contradictions for the characters and prompting emotional responses that give the reader a glimpse into their minds and feelings. Agnes Grey's homesickness and loneliness is one example.

Chapter 13, 'The Primroses', opens with Agnes describing a typical journey home from church. Rosalie Murray must go twice to church on a Sunday, in order to catch as much attention as possible. Walking home is desirable to both Rosalie and Matilda, providing more opportunity for Rosalie to socialise with others on the walk. Agnes describes being completely at the whim of the girls, who may decide to take them with her on their walk or not. She never explicitly mentions her displeasure with the situation, but a current of melancholy runs through the passage in which Agnes details the passive compliancy she must employ. Even the level of thought she must put in to choosing her place in the company while walking seems mentally exhausting:

> As none of the before-mentioned ladies and gentlemen ever noticed me, it was disagreeable to walk beside them, as if listening to what they said, or wishing to be thought one of them, while they talked over me or across, and if their eyes, in speaking, chanced to fall on me, it seemed as if they looked on vacancy — as if they either did not see me, or were very desirous to make it appear so.
>
> It was disagreeable, too, to walk behind, and thus appear to acknowledge my own inferiority; for, in truth, I considered myself pretty nearly as good as the best of them, and wished them to know that I did so, and not to

> imagine that I looked upon myself as a mere domestic, who knew her own place too well to walk beside such fine ladies and gentlemen as they were... though her young ladies might choose to have her with them, and even condescend to converse with her, when no better company were at hand.[3]

Anne makes Agnes's frustration palpable. It's clear to the reader that Agnes is missing her home, and the agreeable companionship to be found there. But instead of having Agnes say simply that she was homesick, Anne uses her ability to write emotively about nature to give Agnes's feelings a greater richness, allowing them to be teased out in a way that makes them more relatable. Agnes describes one particular walk home from church, the ladies accompanied by two young gentlemen humorously described as 'Captain Somebody and Lieutenant Somebody Else (a couple of military fops)':

> Such a party was highly agreeable to Rosalie; but not finding it equally suitable to my taste, I presently fell back, and began to botanise and entomologise along the green banks and budding hedges, till the company was considerably in advance of me, and misanthropy began to melt away beneath the soft, pure air and genial sunshine; but sad thoughts of early childhood, and yearnings for departed joys, or for a brighter future lot, arose instead.[4]

Agnes's exercise of recognising and naming the flora and fauna along the roadside offers her some relief from thinking about her present company. But the practice gradually reminds her of doing the same things in her childhood, and she begins to feel homesick.

> As my eyes wandered over the steep banks covered with young grass and green-leaved plants, and surmounted by nodding hedges, I longed intensely for some familiar flower that might recall the woody dales or green hill-sides of home — the brown moorlands, of course, were out of the question. Such a discovery would make my eyes gush out with water, no doubt; but that was one of my greatest enjoyments now.
>
> At length, I descried, high up between the twisted roots of an oak, three lovely primroses, peeping so sweetly from their hiding place that the tears already started at the sight, but they grew so high above me, that I tried in vain to gather one or two, to dream over and to carry with me; I could not reach them unless I climbed the bank, which I was deterred from doing by hearing a footstep at that moment behind me, and was, therefore, about to turn away, when I was startled by the words, 'Allow me to gather them for you, Miss Grey,' spoken in the grave, low tones of a well-known voice.'[5]

Agnes longs to see a familiar sight from home, knowing that it will evoke in her feelings of homesickness. She says that this sadness is 'one of my greatest enjoyments now', which makes me think she is describing a kind of nostalgia. Anyone who has moved away from their childhood home, their friends, or from a job they loved, can empathise with Agnes's feelings here. Just the sight of something from that idealised past can cause a sad sensation that isn't entirely unenjoyable. A reminder of the past, or a promise of a better future. For Agnes, that trigger of nostalgia is the primroses. It is fitting, then, that the familiar voice offering to pick the flowers for her is Edward Weston, Agnes's future husband.

In this one passage, Anne conveys Agnes's feelings, shows us her coping mechanisms, and also how those mechanisms can lead to intense nostalgia for her home and her family. At the end, she links the joy of home with the man who will be her future husband. Passages like this are to be found all the way through *Agnes Grey*. In my opinion, they give some validation to George Moore's statement that *Agnes Grey* is 'the most perfect prose narrative in English letters'.

This use of nature to provide an unachievable idyll, and evoking responses to nature from characters is used in *The Tenant of Wildfell Hall* too. Chapter 25 of *Wildfell Hall*, 'First Absence', sees Helen alone at Grassdale while she waits for Arthur to return from London. He insists that he will be there for no more than a week; the week slowly turns into a month, and Helen is left alone in the house, her only friend and neighbour currently absent from the area. At the beginning of the chapter, while still in London, Helen was looking forward to being back home in the fresh air at Grassdale. But once she is there, without her husband and almost completely alone, the idyll of the countryside fails to move her if she can't share it with her husband. She laments the slipping away of summer, and how she had looked forward to enjoying it together with Arthur, hoping that maybe it would help her to elevate his mind. She follows this hope with one of the longest sentences in the book, a long, rambling train-of-thought that mixes her joy at nature with the despair of her loneliness:

> But now, — at evening, when I see the round, red sun sink quietly down behind those woody hills, leaving them sleeping in a warm, red, golden haze, I only think another lovely day is lost to him and me; — and at morning, when roused by the flutter and chirp of the sparrows,

and the gleeful twitter of the swallows — all intent upon feeding their young, and full of life and joy in all their own little frames — I open the window to inhale the balmy, soul-reviving air, and look out upon the lovely landscape, laughing in dew and sunshine, — I too often shame that glorious scene with tears of thankless misery, because *he* cannot feel its freshening influence; — and when I wander in the ancient woods, and meet the little wildflowers smiling in my path, or sit in the shadow of our noble ash-trees by the waterside, with their branches gently swaying in the light summer breeze that murmurs through their feathery foliage — my ears full of that low music mingled with the dreamy hum of insects, my eyes abstractedly gazing on the glassy surface of the little lake before me, with the tress that crowd about its bank, some high above, but stretching their wide arms over its margin, all faithfully mirrored far, far down in its glassy depth — though sometimes the images are partially broken by the shirt of aquatic insects, and sometimes, for a

'Country Scene With Cattle', 1836, drawn by Anne at Roe Head.

> moment, the whole is shivered into trembling fragments by a transient breeze that swept the surface too roughly, — still I have no pleasure; for the greater the happiness that nature sets before me, the more I lament that *he* is not here to taste it: the greater the bliss we might enjoy together, the more I feel our present wretchedness apart (yes, ours; he must be wretched, though he may not know it); and the more my senses are pleased, the more my heart is oppressed; for he keeps it with him confined amid the dust and smoke of London, — perhaps, shut up within the walls of his own abominable club.[6]

It reads like a sad and hopeless diary entry, with colons and dashes and unconventional punctuation giving it the sense that it's been written by someone constantly distracted by their emotional state. Helen can see all of the beautiful signs of summer around her and describes them in such as way as to imply that usually these scenes would bring her joy. She uses romantic language, like that used by William Wordsworth, to describe the sights, sounds and sensations of being in and around nature. And yet she fails to be touched by it, except to feel the pain of separation even more deeply.

This sense of being separated from a beautiful ideal is something that appears in Anne's poetry too. In 'Home', the narrator acknowledges the beauty of their current situation but finds it wanting when compared to that which they love best, the scenery of their old home:

> How brightly glistening in the sun
>   The woodland ivy plays!
> While yonder beeches from their barks
>   Reflect his silver rays.

That sun surveys a lovely scene
From softly smiling skies;
And wildly through unnumbered trees
The wind of winter sighs:

Now loud, it thunders o'er my head,
And now in distance dies.
But give me back my barren hills
Where colder breezes rise:

Where scarce the scattered, stunted trees
Can yield an answering swell,
But where a wilderness of heath
Returns the sound as well.

For yonder garden, fair and wide,
With groves of evergreen,
Long winding walks, and orders trim,
And velvet lawns between;

Restore to me that little spot,
With grey walls compassed round,
Where knotted grass neglected lies,
And weeds usurp the ground.

Though all around this mansion high
Invites the foot to roam,
And though its halls are fair within —
Oh, give me back my home![7]

The mansion that is currently home for the narrator, with its fair gardens, velvet lawns and long walks, is no match for the narrator's true home, with its 'knotted grass' and overgrown weeds. Presumably the 'little spot, / with grey walls compassed round' was Haworth parsonage, and the 'barren hills' the moors, as this poem can't be classed as one of the Gondal poems.

When Agnes is trying to reach the primroses, she is looking for flowers that remind her of home, to evoke that feeling of nostalgia in her. Anne achieves almost the same thing in 'The Bluebell':

> But when I looked upon the bank
> My wandering glances fell
> Upon a little trembling flower,
> A single sweet bluebell.
>
> Whence came that rising in my throat,
> That dimness in my eye?
> Why did those burning drops distil —
> Those bitter feelings rise?
>
> O, that lone flower recalled to me
> My happy childhood's hours
> When bluebells seemed like fairy gifts
> A prize among the flowers,
>
> Those sunny days of merriment
> When heart and soul were free,
> And when I dwelt with kindred hearts
> That loved and cared for me.[8]

Flowers appear as central objects in Anne's poetry, and they are also used in her novels to convey almost hidden messages. At the time Anne was writing, the language of flowers had become very fashionable in Victorian society – different flowers had different meanings and could be used as symbols. In the scene in *Agnes Grey* in which Mr Weston gathers some hard-to-reach primroses for Agnes, he continues to walk with her for a while and asks her about flowers:

> 'I like wild flowers,' said he, 'others I don't care about, because I have no particular associations connected with them – except one or two. What are your favourite flowers?'
>
> 'Primroses, blue-bells, and heath-blossoms.'
>
> 'Not violets?'
>
> 'No; because, as you say, I have no particular associations connected with them; for there are no sweet violets among the hills and valleys round my home.'[9]

Contemporary readers may have recognised in this passage the use of particular flowers. Primroses symbolised early youth and first love, and feelings of 'I cannot live without you'. Agnes must have been oblivious to this, otherwise she may have been overwhelmed by Mr Weston's picking them for her. Violets symbolised modesty and faithfulness, while Agnes's other favourite flowers, bluebells, were symbols of humility, constancy and gratitude.[10] The chapter ends with a clue about the future of Agnes and Mr Weston's future: 'As for the primroses, I kept two of them in a glass in my room until they were completely withered, and the housemaid threw them out, and the petals of the other, I pressed between the leaves of my Bible – I have them still, and mean to keep them always.'[11] The first love of her early youth lives in her Bible.

Later in the book, while walking with Matilda, Agnes comes across Mr Weston. They speak for a while and then Mr Weston leaves. Agnes assumes that he is gone and she won't see him again that day, but he returns shortly afterwards 'from the execution of his mission, whatever it might be. He carried in his hand a cluster of beautiful bluebells, which he offered to me, observing, with a smile, that though he had seen so little of me for the last two months, he had not forgotten that bluebells were numbered among my favourite flowers.'[12] To Agnes, the unseen governess, this simple act of remembrance is very significant.

Helen Graham in *Wildfell Hall* also uses the language of flowers to express her love. By the end of the book, she has become a wealthy heiress, higher in station than Gilbert Markham, but she still wishes to marry him. After a long time apart, during which time Helen has been caring for her dying husband, the two are reunited. Initially unsure of how to act towards each other, Helen takes the initiative and tries to let Gilbert know of her intentions. In easily one of the most romantic scenes I've ever read, Helen conveys her feelings towards Gilbert by handing him a rose loaded with meaning:

> 'Do you mean to maintain that you have the same regard for me that you had when last we met?'
>
> 'I have, but it would be wrong to talk of it now.'
>
> 'It was wrong to talk of it *then*, Gilbert; it would *not* now – unless to do so would be to violate the truth.'
>
> I was too much agitated to speak; but, without waiting for an answer, she turned away her glistening eye and crimson cheek, and threw up the window and looked out, whether to calm her own excited feelings or to relieve her embarrassment, – or only to pluck that beautiful half-blown Christmas rose that grew upon the little shrub without, just peeping from the snow, that had hitherto, no doubt, defended it from the frost, and was

> now melting away in the sun. Pluck it, however, she did, and having gently dashed the glittering powder from its leaves, approached it to her lips and said, –
>
> 'This rose is not so fragrant as a summer flower, but it has stood through hardships none of *them* could bear: the cold rain of winter has sufficed to nourish it, and its faint sun to warm it; the bleak winds have not blanched it, or broken its stem, and the keen frost has not blighted it. Look, Gilbert, it is still fresh and blooming as a flower can be, with the cold snow even now on its petals. – Will you have it?'[13]

Helen places the rose in Gilbert's palm. In the language of flowers, the Christmas rose symbolising Helen's heart means 'tranquillise my anxiety'.[14] The reader will also be aware of the other meaning that Helen wishes to convey here; her own heart is no longer in its summer and, like the Christmas-rose, has withstood many punishments and dangers. Helen's heart has been starved of affection, but, just like the rose, it is 'still fresh and blooming as a flower can be, with the cold snow even on its petals'. Gilbert is shocked into silence. Misinterpreting his silence as reluctance to accept her message, Helen takes the rose and throws it back outside. Thankfully the misunderstanding is rectified quickly, and Gilbert retrieves the rose and presses it to his lips.

It is not only flowers that have meaning in Anne's work – nature in general also acts as a metaphor. Gilbert Markham describes the once-great garden of Wildfell Hall near the beginning of the book as 'untilled and untrimmed, abandoned to the weeds and the grass, to the frost and the wind, the rain and the drought'.[15] The garden's fall into disrepair mirrors the downfall of Helen's ancestors and Helen's own situation.[16] Her life has fallen into disrepair just like the garden; both are part of Wildfell Hall, and both used to be able to boast of the wealth that was represented by their appearance.

Over the course of Helen's stay at the hall, she begins to make improvements to the garden, helped along by Gilbert and his family. His sister Rose gives him a small rose tree to give to Helen, which she plants and which Gilbert uses as an excuse to visit her:

> 'Yes; I should like to see your improvements in the garden.'
>
> 'And how your sister's roots have prospered in my charge,' added she, as she opened the gate.
>
> And we sauntered through the garden, and talked of the flowers, the trees, and the book, - and then of other things. The evening was kind and genial, and so was my companion. By degrees, I waxed more warm and tender than, perhaps, I had ever been before; but still I said nothing tangible, and she attempted no repulse; until, in passing a moss rose-tree that I had brought her some weeks since, in my sister's name, she plucked a beautiful half open bud and bade me give it to Rose.
>
> 'May I not keep it myself?' I asked.
>
> 'No; but here is another for you.'[17]

This is the first instance of Helen handing Gilbert a rose from her garden. But where the Christmas rose was in full bloom, this one is but a half-open bud. Helen is not yet ready to allow herself to surrender her whole heart to Gilbert. In planting the rose tree, and making improvements to the garden, Helen is in a sense asserting the control she intends to take back of her own life.

Nature found its way into Anne's art as well as her writing.

While it is usually Branwell who is considered the artist of the family, all the Brontës enjoyed drawing and painting, and a number of Anne's drawings and paintings have survived. There are portraits of children (perhaps based on her pupils), portraits of women, and a portrait that has 'a very bad picture' written on the back has been suggested to be a self-portrait. I especially like Anne's drawings of the countryside and natural landscapes. Her elm tree illustration, with its tiny flock of birds in the background, is highly detailed. Anne sketched Little Ouseburn church, the church that she went to with the Robinsons when she was governess at Thorp Green, and she also sketched Roe Head.

The drawing titled 'What you please' was produced by Anne in 1840, and shows a young woman walking through a wood. The woman has classically attractive features, set in a serious-looking expression. She is leaning on a tree with her left hand, and gently pushing aside a smaller branch with her right. Edward Chitham suggests that the title came from Mrs Robinson's instruction, 'You may do what you please, Miss Brontë', and so the drawing depicts just that – a young woman, like Anne, doing what she pleases. Chitham also notes the 'harmony of the girl with her surroundings. Her creator sees human nature as part of Nature itself (a view shared by Emily).'[18]

ANNE AND ANIMALS

Reading Anne and Emily's Diary Papers gives a bit of an idea of how many animals lived at the parsonage over the years. The first Diary Paper, from 1834, begins, 'I fed Rainbow, Diamond, Snowflake, jasper pheasent [sic] alias this morning.'[19] Rainbow, Diamond and Snowflake were doves that lived in the dovecot in the courtyard behind the parsonage.[20]

Anne's Diary Paper from 30 July 1841 includes a section about the new animals in the parsonage and what has happened to them. She refers to Keeper (Emily's dog), a 'sweet little cat' that disappeared, a hawk (Emily's merlin hawk, Nero, which she rescued and nursed back to health) and geese.[21]

Animals were a large part of daily life at the parsonage, loved and looked after by the whole family. So important were the pets that Ellen Nussey wrote about them in her *Reminiscences*:

> During Miss Branwell's [Aunt Branwell] reign at the parsonage, the love of animals had to be kept in due subjection. There was then but one dog, which was admitted to the parlour at stated times. Emily and Anne always gave him a portion of their breakfast, which was, by their own choice, the old north country diet of oatmeal porridge. Later on, there were three household pets — the tawny, strong-limbed 'Keeper', Emily's favourite: he was so completely under her control, she could quite easily make him spring and roar like a lion. She taught him this kind of occasional play without any coercion. 'Flossy', — long, silky-haired, black and white 'Flossy.' — was Anne's favourite; and black 'Tom', the tabby, was everybody's favourite. It received such gentle treatment it seemed to have lost cat's nature, and subsided into luxurious amiability and contentment. The Brontës' love of dumb creatures made them very sensitive of the treatment bestowed upon them. For any one to offend in this respect was with them an infallible bad sign, and a blot on the disposition.[22]

Anne's dog Flossy had been given to her by the Robinson girls at Thorp Green and became a fixture at the parsonage.

Charlotte painted her portrait twice, and both Flossy and Keeper appear in letters (Anne writes of Flossy being 'fatter than ever' in one letter to Ellen[23]). There's no doubt that they were treated as members of the family, fed from the table and invited to sit on sofas. The animals at the parsonage were well loved. Moreover, kindness to animals was such a huge mark of a person's character that Anne included it extensively in her two novels.

The most infamous account of animals in *Agnes Grey* is the death of the baby birds. Tom Bloomfield is one of Agnes's pupils at Wellwood House. He first shows Miss Grey his bird and mole traps. Agnes asks what he does with the birds once he catches them, and he says very matter-of-factly that '"Sometimes I give them to the cat; sometimes I cut them in pieces with my pen-knife; but the next, I mean to roast alive."'[24] Tom is completely comfortable with the extreme violence that he carries out against the birds. Later, when his Uncle Robson gives him a nest full of newly hatched chicks, Agnes decides to kill the baby birds all at once rather than let Tom have his way with them. The boy is disappointed, and Agnes is distraught. 'Loud were the outcries, terrible the execrations consequent upon this daring outrage; Uncle Robson had been coming up the walk with his gun, and was, just then, pausing to kick his dog. Tom flew towards him, vowing he would make him kick me instead of Juno.'[25]

Flossy, painted by Emily.

Uncle Robson, on the way to kick his dog, is not a character that we should like. He gave the birds to Tom, knowing that he would torture them. This encouragement of violence, passed down from fathers and uncles to the young boys in the family, was something that Anne was to return to later in *Wildfell Hall* (see Chapter Six).

Another example in *Agnes Grey* of behaviour towards animals revealing a person's true nature is Mr Edward Weston's reaction to a cat jumping on his knee: he strokes the animal and smiles, which is 'a good sign'. In contrast, Mr Hatfield 'knocked her off, like as it might be in scorn or anger, poor thing'.[26]

Matilda Murray is another character whose treatment of animals does not come across well. She buys a little dog named Snap, but resents it when it becomes more attached to Agnes:

> At my feet lay a little rough terrier. It was the property of Miss Matilda; but she hated the animal, and intended to sell it, alleging that it was quite spoiled. It was really an excellent dog of its kind; but she affirmed it was fit for nothing, and had not even the sense to know its own mistress.
>
> The fact was she had purchased it when but a small puppy, insisting at first that no one should touch it but herself; but soon becoming tired of so helpless and troublesome a nursling, she had gladly yielded to my entreaties to be allowed to take charge of it; and I, by carefully nursing the little creature from infancy to adolescence, of course, had obtained its affections: a reward I should have greatly valued, and looked upon as far outweighing all the trouble I had had with it, had not poor Snap's grateful feelings exposed him to many a harsh word and many a spiteful kick and pinch from his owner, and were he not now in danger of being 'put away' in consequence, or transferred to some rough, stony-hearted master. But how could I help it? I could not make the dog hate me by cruel treatment, and she would not propitiate him by kindness.[27]

Rather than give the dog to Agnes, Matilda sells Snap to a local rat-catcher out of spite. Snap and Agnes are reunited in the end, however, after Snap is saved by none other than Mr Weston.

In *Wildfell Hall*, once again the treatment of animals can be used almost to foreshadow events. Eliza Millward's older sister Mary, for example, is described as 'a plain, quiet, sensible girl, who had patiently nursed their mother, through her last long, tedious illness, and been the housekeeper, and family drudge, from thence to the present time'. Less attractive than her sister Eliza, much quieter and serious, she was 'trusted and valued by her father, loved and courted by all dogs, cats, children, and poor people, and slighted and neglected by everybody else'.[28] Gilbert pays her almost no attention and assumes, from her appearance, that there is nothing to her. But Mary goes on to make one of the best marital matches in the book, surprising everyone except those readers who noticed that she was well-loved by animals, children and poor people. Being kind to animals was equated with having empathy for anyone who could not defend themselves or was vulnerable in some way.

Arthur Huntingdon, Helen's abusive husband, is unkind to animals. He spends one particularly sulky afternoon alternately petting and teasing his dogs in a childish manner. Bored of that, he returns to find Helen occupied with a book. He stretches out on a sofa and tries to sleep:

> But his favourite cocker, Dash, that had been lying at my feet, took the liberty of jumping upon him and beginning to lick his face. He struck it off with a smart blow; and the poor dog squeaked and ran cowering back to me. When he woke up, about half an hour after, he called it to him again, but Dash only looked sheepish and wagged the tip of his tail. He called again more sharply, but Dash only

> clung the closer to me, and licked my hand, as if imploring protection. Enraged at this, his master snatched up a heavy book and hurled it at his head. The poor dog set up a piteous outcry, and ran to the door. I let him out, and then quietly took up the book.
>
> 'Give that book to me,' said Arthur, in no very courteous tone. I gave it to him.
>
> 'Why did you let the dog out?' he asked; 'you knew I wanted him.'
>
> 'By what token?' I replied; 'by your throwing the book at him? but perhaps it was intended for me?'[29]

It is almost two centuries since Anne was making the treatment of animals a defining trait of her characters. The Royal Society of the Prevention of Cruelty to Animals was established when Anne was just two years old. Its founding reflected a growing interest in the welfare of animals, and Anne joined the ranks of women such as Mary Wollstonecraft, Sarah Trimmer and Mary Sherwood, who all wrote about the importance of showing kindness towards animals.[30]

In the last few years there has been an increase in the amount of fiction, mostly from Japan, about cats. *The Guest Cat* by Takashi Hiraide came out in the UK in 2014, and tells the story of how one couple's life is affected by a cat that comes to visit. Since then, there has been *The Travelling Cat Chronicles* by Hiro Arikawa, and *If Cats Disappeared From The World* by Genki Kawamura. The main character in Kawamura's story is incredibly unlikeable, until we learn how much his cat means to him. Tales of kindness towards animals will never go away, and it makes Anne more endearing to know that she was part of a long tradition of encouraging this kindness.

SCARBOROUGH AND THE SEA

Even before her visit to Scarborough as governess to the Robinson children, Anne had loved the idea of the sea. A drawing of hers, dated 13 November 1839, depicts a young woman shielding her eyes as she looks out at a sunrise or a sunset over the sea. The first time I saw it, I assumed that Emily or Charlotte must have drawn it. After all, they were more forward-facing than Anne, and at least Charlotte was more ambitious, or so I had been led to believe. The young woman stands on a cliff, as the sun's rays extend all the way across the distant horizon. The miniature boat in the distance gives some sense of scale. It's a picture, to me, of someone looking towards a bright future, expansive and unpredictable as the ocean. She may be shielding her eyes, but her posture suggests that she is unafraid of things to come. In November 1839, Anne was a month away from being dismissed from her first governess position. She was struggling with the children and may have been trying to find a new post, a way to improve her prospects and move on to better things.

It's an image that is discordant with the one generally associated with Anne. Is this a drawing that could have been produced by someone who wished to hide away from the world, someone whose outlook was shadowed by religious melancholy? It shocked me that someone I'd always believed to be so shy, who lived in the shadow of her sisters, could create such a hopeful image.

The Robinsons, when visiting Scarborough, stayed in furnished rooms in the best part of town, 'the Spa'. Wood's Lodgings are located in a Georgian terrace that overlooks the South Bay. From its position on the cliff top, Anne would have been able to see the beaches and the castle on the headland. Anne loved this place so much that she chose to stay in Wood's Lodgings with Charlotte and Ellen when they went to Scarborough during Anne's final illness. It was there that she died, having been able to visit the sea for the last time.

Anne's poem, published in 1846 as 'Lines Composed In A Wood On A Windy Day', expresses some of her feelings about the sea:

My soul is awakened, my spirit is soaring,
And carried aloft on the wings of the breeze;
For, above, and around me, the wild wind is roaring
Arousing to rapture the earth and the seas.

The long withered grass in the sunshine is glancing,
The bare trees are tossing their branches on high;
The dead leaves beneath them are merrily dancing,
The white clouds are scudding across the blue sky.

I wish I could see how the ocean is lashing
The foam of its billows to whirlwinds of spray,
I wish I could see how its proud waves are dashing
And hear the wild roar of their thunder today![31]

'Sunrise over Sea', 1839, perhaps a self-portrait by Anne.

In *Agnes Grey*, Anne sends her heroine to live next to the sea, in a fictional town based on Scarborough, to run a school with her mother. Though the school was far from the beach itself, Agnes took every opportunity she could to visit the sea:

> [...] the sea was my delight; and I would often gladly pierce the town to obtain the pleasure of a walk beside it, whether with the pupils, or alone with my mother during the vacations. It was delightful to me at all times and seasons, but especially in the wild commotion of a rough sea-breeze, and in the brilliant freshness of a summer morning.[32]

The sea is also present in *Wildfell Hall*. As their friendship begins to grow, Helen asks Gilbert if it is true that their village is situated not far from the sea. She wished to paint it, and as a result, a party made up of Gilbert's family and friends accompanies Helen and her young son to the cliffs. It is there that Gilbert begins to realise the strength of his feelings for Helen, noticing how beautiful she is as she beholds the 'glorious scene' before her: 'She said nothing: but she stood still, and fixed her eyes upon it with a gaze that assured me she was not disappointed.'[33]

Helen's stance in this passage reminds me of the woman looking out to sea in Anne's sketch. And the scene is made all the more beautiful for Helen and Gilbert's appreciation of the natural beauty they are surrounded by.

Anne even spent some time on Scarborough's beach just days before her death, such was her love of the seashore. It's safe to assume that she spent as much time on the beach as she could when she was at Scarborough with the Robinsons, and Anne's collection of beach pebbles is still held at the Brontë Parsonage Museum. It's an activity that humanises an almost mythical figure: shadowy sister of Charlotte and Emily Brontë, author of one of the most intense scrutinies of women's rights in the nineteenth century... and pebble collector. 2018 saw the republication of Clarence Ellis's *The Pebbles On The Beach*, and in 2019, *The Book of Pebbles* by Christopher Stocks and Angie Lewin was published. The popularity of these books shows that it is still a fascination that many people share, and knowing that it's something Anne Brontë also did seems to make her more relatable, more reachable.

As we've seen, Anne used nature in her writing as a method of describing character, to set scenes, and to convey hidden meanings without the need for dialogue or direct descriptions. Knowing to look out for these signs can enhance the meaning of certain scenes, increasing their power and making them last in the memory. One of the most memorable scenes for me is when Agnes is finally reunited with Edward Weston.

She arrives at the beach early one morning and takes joy at being the first person there. She soon spots a gentleman with a dog, but turns her attention away from them and back towards the sea:

> But however interesting such a scene might be, I could not wait to witness it, for the sun and the sea so dazzled my eyes in that direction, that I could but afford one glance; and then I turned again to delight myself with the sight and sound of the sea dashing against my promontory – with no prodigious force, for the swell was broken by the tangled sea-weed and the unseen rocks beneath; otherwise I should soon have been deluged with spray. [...]
>
> Presently, I heard a snuffling sound behind me, and then a dog came frisking and wriggling to my feet. It was my own Snap – the little dark, wire-haired terrier! When I spoke his name, he leapt up in my face, and yelled for joy.

> Almost as much delighted as himself, I caught the little creature in my arms, and kissed him repeatedly. But how came he to be there? He could not have dropped from the sky, or come all that way alone: it must be either his master, the rat-catcher, or somebody else that had brought him; so, repressing my extravagant caresses, and endeavouring to repress likewise, I looked round, and beheld – Mr Weston![34]

Their reunion takes place by the sea, and not only is it a reunion between Agnes and Edward, but also between Agnes and her beloved dog. It's the Anne Brontë double-whammy – a well-loved pet and the romance of the sea. Add to that the fact that Edward Weston took the dog under his own protection, and it's no surprise that Agnes married him.

Their engagement, too, is set by the sea. Agnes and Edward head out for a walk after a thunder shower, which had 'certainly had a most beneficial effect upon the weather, and the evening was most delightful'. It's a simple observation on Anne's part, but immediately you can feel the kind of evening that they're heading out into: vivid colours, dramatic skies, ideal romantic conditions. They reach a hill overlooking the sea, and Edward sees that '"by those light clouds in the west, there will be a brilliant sunset, and we shall be in time to witness its effect upon the sea, at the most moderate rate of progression"'.[35] Anne painted beautiful scenes by describing those elements of nature that brought her the most joy, and the genuine portrayal of Anne's own feelings about those elements of nature that she most loved is what gives those scenes their power.

FIVE

ANNE AND RELIGION

Anne Brontë's name and reputation are almost synonymous with the word 'piety'. In conversations with friends and family about the Brontës, most of them at some point have said, 'Wasn't Anne the really religious one?' The way in which they ask this gives me some indication of why, even if they have read *Jane Eyre* and *Wuthering Heights*, they haven't read anything by Anne. There's an assumption being made here about the quality of Anne's books, which is based on the fact that she was religious and had a strong Christian faith. The expectation seemed to be that because she was religious, because her books grapple with ideas about faith more than her sisters' works do, her work is somehow sombre and dull, maybe even depressing.

This image of a restrictive religious seriousness was, in part, propelled by Charlotte's 'Biographical Notice' to *Wuthering Heights* and *Agnes Grey*. In it, she writes that Anne inhabits her own world, almost completely cut off from everyone else. Charlotte inserts a physical barrier between Anne and the rest of humanity when she writes that Anne's mind and feeling were covered with a 'nun-like veil'.[1] Charlotte also wrote that Anne was 'a very sincere and practical Christian, but the tinge of religious melancholy communicated a sad shade to her brief, blameless life'.[2] In describing her sister this way, Charlotte was again very cleverly depicting Anne as someone outside of blame – someone who strove to be a good Christian, who possibly had little room for anything else in her life.

Unfortunately, Charlotte's depiction of her youngest sister has once again had an unfair and long-lasting effect. The prospect of reading a novel tinged with 'religious melancholy' was one of the things that put me off reading Anne for a long time, as I imagine it has been for many other potential readers. And yet, when I finally dedicated some time to Anne's novels and poems, this representation of Anne was just another myth to be blown out of the water. Part of my mission, therefore, is to expose an Anne who is often far from melancholy. Even when characters are going through a crisis, or the narrator of a poem is feeling despondent, Anne always introduces an element of hope. The reader rarely gets the feeling that Anne is being bleak for the sake of it, or to shock the audience. The depressions sometimes experienced by her characters are very firmly rooted in reality, and as such are subtle, complex and (most importantly) can be overcome.

The critic Lucy Hughes-Hallett wrote the introduction to the 2012 edition of the Everyman's Library publication of Anne's two novels. In it, she provides a brief and effective summary of how Anne's religion affected her works, while acknowledging that it might make reading Anne difficult for modern readers:

> […] her religious faith wasn't of the meek-and-mild variety; rather it gives her fiction a fiery edge. She earnestly believed in the rewards and punishment of the Christian vision of the afterlife. When her characters – ignorant cottager or reckless gentleman alike – become frantic with fear of damnation, they are not thinking metaphorically. They are taking scriptural warning as literally, and seriously, as the author herself did. Such a way of thinking is alien to many twenty-first-century readers, but Anne Brontë wasn't a bigot. She was morally rigorous, but she was also tolerant. She persuaded herself that redemption was offered to all. Her understanding of psychology is subtle. She refuses to reduce any of her characters, however ill-behaved, to the simple status of out-and-out-villain.[3]

These ideas are worth exploring more fully, in order to get to grips with the *real* Anne Brontë. What were Anne's beliefs, and how did her relationship with religion help her to construct believable, multi-dimensional characters? What do Anne's characters tell us about Anne's morals, and how she tried to apply them to daily life?

I approached Anne's books knowing that there was a strong chance I wasn't going to agree with her views on religion. I was also almost completely ignorant of the ways in which the religious landscape of the UK has changed over the last two hundred years – the most I knew was that attending church and studying the Bible was much more popular and taken more seriously than it is today. We don't have room here to discuss it in the detail it deserves, but acknowledging the religious changes, and the atmosphere surrounding religion in which the Brontës grew up, can have a big effect on how you read anything by Anne – it is entirely possible to enjoy her novels and poems without any knowledge of the role religion played at that point in history, but having that context can give a greater appreciation for Anne's thoughtful approach to writing, and her analytical nature.

One of the important things to remember when discussing religion and the Brontës is that the language of the time would have been heavily influenced by the language of the Bible. 'Religious texts were the central texts of the West and they begat the language of the West,' writes John Maynard. 'One has only to see Brontë characters bandying replies from the Bible or Church tradition to see how much their language and ways of thought ride upon those of religious tradition.'[4] In a scene in *Wildfell Hall* where Helen tries to convince her aunt that Arthur Huntingdon is a worthy man to marry, both of them speak to each other almost entirely in biblical references. Even Huntingdon makes references to Bible passages, but when he speaks them, they are often wrong, or changed to fit his needs.

Learning more about Anne's Christian upbringing, and the attitudes to religion at the time that Anne was writing, allowed me to find ways to relate to what Anne was writing about. The more I became familiar with Anne's works, the more I realised that she did have a lot to say that I could identify with, even when following a Christian theme. Her religious philosophy seemed to be based on the idea that everyone is worthy of forgiveness, as Lucy Hughes-Hallett observed when she wrote that Anne didn't just write a character to be an 'out-and-out villain'.

A CHRISTIAN BACKDROP

In the twenty-first century, it's very easy for us to forget just how far-reaching the influence of the Anglican Church was back in the nineteenth century, especially for the Brontës. Having a father in the Church made religion a central part of their lives, even if they weren't consciously aware of it all the time. It influenced every part of their family's history: from the family's relocation to Haworth, to the unfortunate decision to send the eldest Brontë children to the Clergy Daughters' School at Cowan Bridge (see Chapter One).

But it would be unfair to think that the religious backdrop into which the Brontës were born was completely negative, however. Patrick's friends were made up of men he had met as a student at Cambridge, and clergymen he worked with and admired. Their mother Maria also immersed herself in parish life.

Patrick Brontë was a member of the Church of England at a time when there wasn't much of a division between church and state. For example, in order to attend Oxford or Cambridge University, you had to be a member of the Anglican Church. This only ended in 1871 with the Universities Tests Act, which meant that Dissenters, Non-Conformists, Roman Catholics and non-Christians were allowed to become students at or be employed by Oxford, Cambridge and Durham universities. Dissenters and Non-Conformists were also Christian groups, but they didn't practise the same beliefs and traditions as the Anglican Church. They included groups like the Baptists, Calvinists, Methodists and Moravians. Of course, the Baptist and Methodist movements are still well known today, and it's difficult to imagine a time when being associated with either of these churches would have been controversial.

Patrick himself was an Evangelical Anglican. Evangelism placed a great emphasis on a life dedicated to God: followers were encouraged to be self-reflective, and to be aware of their own capacity for sin. The Day of Judgement and the threat of eternal punishment were very real, and Evangelical ministers preached the importance of living a life in the duty of God. This isn't to suggest that Patrick was anything like the self-important Mr Hatfield from *Agnes Grey*; on the contrary, living a life in the duty of God for Patrick meant working to improve the lives of everyone around him. Some of his politics were particularly progressive for the time, such as his opinions on the criminal justice system. It was the law to condemn a man to death for stealing a sheep, but Patrick posed questions about a man's reasons for breaking the law. To Patrick, the sin wasn't purely the act of stealing, but a system that would let a man go hungry and condemn him for taking desperate actions to alleviate the hunger of his family.

His liberal views were applied to his family too; there was no reason why his daughters shouldn't have access to the education he gave to Branwell. He took an interest in their daily lives, as when he gave them a mask to remove their self-consciousness, and when he wrote 'By my daughter Charlotte' on one of Charlotte's portraits of Anne. When Elizabeth was sent home ill from school, the very next day he travelled to Cowan Bridge to collect Charlotte and Emily himself. He treated his children as people, recognising and taking joy in their individual personalities and encouraging their interests, and talking to them about things children at the time wouldn't have been expected to understand.

Anne would have grown up being very aware that, for Christians, a life of sin would have resulted in everlasting punishment in the afterlife. However, her father's influence and his clear questioning of authority when it came to helping his fellow man fostered an environment in which Anne felt free to question the teachings that she began to doubt. Patrick's emphasis on education possibly even inspired Anne's desire to study her Bible in the pursuit of answers to her questions.

Beyond her father, Anne's Aunt Branwell also had an influence on her religious views. Anne 'was her Aunt's favourite', according to Ellen Nussey in her *Reminiscences*. Being so young when her mother died, Anne only really knew Aunt Branwell as the maternal figure in her life, and Anne was therefore the Brontë for whom family life was the most stable – and this becomes apparent in reading the Brontës' works. Anne's depiction of family is the most secure. Agnes Grey is the baby of her family – patronised, but loved and cared for, and eager to prove herself. Gilbert Markham in *Wildfell Hall* lives with his mother, younger sister and brother. The three siblings wind each other up, as siblings often do, but ultimately the family unit is a solid one in which they all look out for each other. Charlotte and Emily, on the other hand, who were old enough to have a recollection of a mother other than Aunt Branwell, filled their books with orphaned, unwanted and neglected children.

Aunt Elizabeth Branwell had originally arrived in Haworth to care for her dying sister, but she ended up staying at the parsonage for the rest of her life. She was well loved by all the Brontës, particularly Branwell and Anne, who spent the most time with her as children while the older girls were away at school. She was responsible for teaching Anne about household duties. Indeed, all the Brontë girls learned, under Aunt Branwell's care, how to take part in boring but necessary household tasks, such as making and mending clothes.

Winifred Gérin acknowledges the love they had for Aunt Branwell, but seems to take Mrs Gaskell's stance that 'the children respected her, and had that sort of affection for her which is generated by esteem; but I do not think they ever freely loved her'.[5] She also lays most of the blame for Anne's apparent religious melancholy on Aunt Branwell, someone who believed that 'hell was very real and damnation certain for the vast majority of mankind'. Gérin states that 'Anne Brontë had early branded on her mind the exhortation from Proverbs 3:9–18: "My child despise not the chastening of the Lord; neither be weary of his correction. For whom the Lord loveth he correcteth, even as a father the son in whom he delighteth."'[6]

This is a very different picture of Aunt Branwell to the one given by Ellen Nussey. Ellen wrote that when she first visited Haworth, 'Miss Branwell (the aunt of the Brontes) took possession of their guest and treated her with the care and solicitude due to a weary traveller'. She was a 'small, antiquated little lady,' a lively member of the parsonage who, rather than ruling through fear, was very capable of communicating on the Brontës' level. Most importantly, Ellen portrays her as someone very capable of having fun:

> She took snuff out of a very pretty gold snuff-box, which she sometimes presented to you with a little laugh, as if she enjoyed the slight shock and astonishment visible

> in your countenance. In summer she spent part of the afternoon in reading aloud to Mr. Bronte. In the winter evenings she must have enjoyed this; for she and Mr. Bronte had often to finish their discussions on what she had read when we all met for tea. She would be very lively and intelligent, and tilt arguments against Mr. Bronte without fear.[7]

Winifred Gérin wrote about Aunt Branwell as if she was a strict Methodist, preaching a doctrine of fear to her young and impressionable niece. Aunt Branwell was a Methodist but, like her sister Maria, she was a Wesleyan Methodist – Wesleyan Methods believed in the essential goodness and mercy of God, and that anyone may get into heaven if they live a good Christian life. Their beliefs were much more in accordance with that of Patrick's Evangelical Anglicanism. Maria and Aunt Branwell both attended Patrick's services, and both chose to have an Anglican burial and funeral service. It is hard to believe that a woman who supposedly held such strict beliefs would be willing to put those to one side to attend an Anglican church service. It's also hard to imagine that Patrick would allow his sister-in-law to preach such extreme beliefs (in comparison to his) to his children.

The branch of Methodism in which Aunt Branwell had been brought up rejected outright Calvinist doctrine. Calvinists believed that the number of people who could enter heaven was finite, and those who could enter had already been predetermined. According to Calvinism, a person would never be able to do enough while alive to secure themselves a place in heaven; there was no hope for them. Only the Elect could enter. While Aunt Branwell, like Anne's father, believed in hell and eternal punishment for sinners, neither of them believed in the Calvinist doctrine that only the Elect went to heaven. Their take on the matter was: lead a good life, reject sin, and you may be in with a chance.

So Aunt Branwell certainly influenced some of Anne's religious beliefs, but those beliefs were more likely to be in line with those of Patrick. Arguably, she may actually have had a bigger influence on Anne's social views. Aunt Branwell's main goal while caring for and teaching Anne may have been to impress upon her the duties that were expected of women: young girls do needlework; young women learn the things most likely to help them when they become wives (housekeeping, sewing and accomplishments that might make them more attractive). And if a girl really must take up a job, then she should train to be a governess. Essentially, learn the skills to be subservient, quiet and humble. However, Anne's books make it clear that she disagrees that women should remain unoccupied and view marriage as their ultimate goal. Aunt Branwell's biggest influence on Anne may have been to unsuspectingly cultivate in her niece a nature that questions authority. Aunt Branwell may have been teaching maidenly modesty, but there's every possibility that Anne was silently questioning her aunt's views regarding a woman's place in society.

As well as her father and Aunt Branwell, there is one other person that had an effect on Anne: William Cowper. He was an eighteenth-century British poet and writer of hymns who became preoccupied with the idea that he was destined for hell (as did Anne), and his poem 'The Castaway' became an especially important work for both Anne and Branwell.[8] It frames the plight of someone who knows that they are not a member of the Calvinist Elect as if they are a castaway in a storm. Anne identified strongly with Cowper's views and doubts, even writing a poem dedicated to him, 'To Cowper':

Sweet are thy strains, Celestial Bard,
    And oft in childhood's years
I've read them o'er and o'er again
    With floods of silent tears.

The language of my inmost heart
    I traced in every line—
My sins, *my* sorrows, hopes and fears
    Were there, and only mine.

The poem begins with the narrator expressing just how strongly they connected and identified with Cowper's words, seeing her own sins, hopes and fears expressed within his poems.

Is He the source of every good,
    The spring of purity?
Then in thine hours of deepest woe
    Thy God was still with thee.

William Cowper.

How else when every hope was fled
    Couldst thou so fondly cling
To holy things and holy men
    And how so sweetly sing—

Of things that God alone could teach?
    And whence that purity;
That hatred of all sinful ways,
    That gentle charity?

Are these the symptoms of a heart
    Of Heavenly grace bereft,
For ever banished from its God,
    To Satan's fury left?

Yet should thy darkest fears be true,
    If Heaven be so severe
That such a soul as thine is lost,
    O! How then shall I appear?[9]

The narrator argues that God surely must have been with Cowper when he wrote, as how else would he have been able to create such poems? Cowper, with all of his doubts and fears, never gave up on his faith or on the goodness of others, and according to the narrator, this means that Cowper must have been loved and led by his God. She takes this further and asserts that surely Cowper must have made it into heaven. And if he didn't, what hope is there for someone like herself?

A RELIGIOUS CRISIS

The fact that Anne related to William Cowper shows that she had her own religious doubts and fears. But where did they come from? What would a young, thoughtful, serious girl like her have to worry about? Surely she can't have worried about sin; there's no evidence that she ever did anything that could be considered sinful (apart from, perhaps, tying children to tables so that she could write). It is more likely that Anne's religious doubts began to become more prominent, and eventually more overwhelming, while she was at Roe Head. It was her first time away from home, and Charlotte was keeping her distance as a teacher. Anne made only one recorded friend at Roe Head, Ann Cook, and she was much younger than Anne (she was ten when Anne met her at Roe Head, aged fifteen).[10] On top of all that, Anne suffered an illness at Roe Head that was so serious it would bring her time at the school to an end.

The environment at Roe Head itself had a very heavily Christian influence. Two of the five Wooler sisters who helped at the school had married clergymen, and Marianne Wooler's husband, the Reverend Thomas Allbutt, was especially strict – he even advised the girls against the evils of dancing.[11] Anne was possibly lonely, very vulnerable, and exposed to more extreme religious views than she was used to.

Anne's father and aunt, an Anglican and a Wesleyan Methodist, believed that eternal punishment was a real possibility. But they also believed in the mercy of God, and that those who lived as good Christians may be able to get into heaven. Anne certainly held the fear of eternal punishment that was instilled in most Christians, but why should she have felt especially fearful of it? It may have been that she often felt her faith wavering. All the Brontë children held a distaste for the idea that Christianity was synonymous with church and church attendance. Both Anne and Charlotte caricatured un-Christian clergymen (Anne's Mr Hatfield from *Agnes Grey*, Charlotte's Mr Helstone and the unruly curates from *Shirley*) and condemned the idea that they should show them reverence just because they were clergymen.[12] When she was younger, Anne may have felt that, in questioning the Church, she was also questioning God.

A wavering faith and disenchantment with formal religion were worries that Anne later gave to her character Nancy Brown in *Agnes Grey*: 'I was sore distressed, Miss Grey [...] when I took my Bible, I could get no comfort of it at all. That very chapter 'at you've just been reading troubled me as much as aught – "He that loveth not, knoweth not God." It seemed fearsome to me; for I felt that I loved neither God nor man as I should do, and could not, if I tried ever so.'[13]

Not only was Anne worried that she might never be able to be a good enough person, she worried for those around her too. She couldn't accept that a loving God would allow for anyone to receive eternal punishment. Her own readings of the Bible had convinced her that this couldn't be the case. This contradicted the teachings of both her aunt and her father, and as such, must have been incredibly confusing. The clergymen associated with the school, and the ones in the wider community of Dewsbury, leaned towards Calvinistic doctrine.[14] If she felt that her views were not in line with the clergymen she was familiar with, it makes sense that she would turn to someone whose views more closely matched her own. And so she asked to see Reverend James La Trobe, the minister and teacher of the Moravian chapel and school at Well House in Mirfield.[15]

James La Trobe shared Anne's views about God and eternal punishment. The Moravians believed in Universal Salvation, which stated that all souls will eventually be saved. Calvinists believed that only a predetermined Elect could get into heaven. The Anglican Church (including Patrick and Aunt Branwell) believed that anyone may be saved, but punishment was still eternal. Universal Salvation was an incredibly controversial belief which stated that everyone, regardless of whether or not they have sinned, will ultimately be redeemed. Yes, they may be punished, but their punishment will not be eternal. After an appropriate amount of time, they too will ascend to heaven.

James La Trobe and his doctrine must have been a great source of comfort to Anne, and he visited her more than once during her illness. He later wrote an account of his experience of meeting her at Roe Head, saying that she was 'very grateful' for his visits and 'her heart opened to the sweet views of salvation'.[16]

Anne returned home in December 1837, back to the comforts of family and the less strict religion of her father. Her belief in Universal Salvation continued to grow, and in her 'Bible Project', completed while at Thorp Green, she highlighted the passages in her Bible that most resonated with those beliefs.[17] It permeated *Wildfell Hall* very heavily, in which even a terrible man like Arthur Huntingdon is encouraged to believe that he, too, will ultimately be saved. And Anne's disdain for the Calvinists was made indisputable by her poem 'A Word to the Calvinists', written in 1843. It was published in 1846 as 'A Word to the "Elect"', possibly in an attempt to be less overt (though the meaning would have been clear to anyone who read it):

> You may rejoice to think yourselves secure,
> You may be grateful for the gift divine,
> That grace unsought which made your black hearts pure
> And fits your earthborn souls in Heaven to shine.

But is it sweet to look around and view
Thousands excluded from that happiness,
Which they deserve at least as much as you,
Their faults not greater nor their virtues less?

Anne asks the Calvinists how they can take pride in being a member of the Elect, knowing that there are others who will suffer despite working hard their whole lives to follow God. She makes the point also that it is nothing to be proud of – they have done nothing to earn their predetermined place in heaven.

Anne continues, arguing that it seems odd to be grateful for the death of Jesus as a Calvinist, 'Because for *all* the Saviour did not die', and asks if their hearts truly 'expand to all mankind'. Anne says that she wouldn't be able to enjoy her place as a member of the Elect knowing that her fellow men were 'doomed to endless misery', saying, 'May God withhold such cruel joy from me!'

The tone and even the style of the poem then change, as Anne writes about her vision – a very thinly disguised description of Universal Salvation:

And O! there lives within my heart
A hope long nursed by me,
(And should its cheering ray depart
How dark my soul would be)

That as in Adam all have died
In Christ shall all men live
And ever round his throne abide
Eternal praise to give;

That even the wicked shall at last

Be fitted for the skies
And when their dreadful doom is past
To light and life arise.[18]

The last two stanzas express Anne's wish that, once their punishment is over and their 'cup of wrath is drained', those who have sinned should realise the error of their ways and join God in heaven. The stanzas above, however, are the most explicit in their conveyance of Anne's belief in Universal Salvation. It's well known that Anne's books, as well as her sisters, were criticised for their coarseness. But it is also the case that Anne's views on Universal Salvation were a source of upset as well. As Marianne Thormählen writes in *Anne Brontë and her Bible*, 'It is impossible to overstate the boldness of Anne's position as regards salvation.' She continues, 'It was one thing to argue [...] that all *may* be saved. It is quite another to assert that all *will ultimately* be saved, through God's mercy and Christ's Atonement.'[19]

RADICAL ANNE

Universal Salvation as a concept was not very widely accepted, and one of the arguments against it was that removing the deterrent of hell would encourage more people to behave wickedly, just because they could. We can see part of this attitude in *Wildfell Hall*, especially in the way Helen's aunt reacts to Helen's own interpretation of the Bible.

In Chapter 20, 'Persistence', Helen's aunt makes it clear that she does not approve of her niece's husband-to-be, Arthur Huntingdon, eventually telling Helen that she will be lonely when she reaches heaven and her husband has gone to hell, to be punished for eternity. Helen can't accept that, and, though she acknowledges that her husband's punishment may be a possibility, she does not believe that it will be eternal:

'And suppose, even, that he should continue to love you, and you him, and that you should pass through life together with tolerable comfort, – how will it be in the end, when you see yourselves parted forever; you, perhaps, taken into eternal bliss, and he cast into the lake that burneth with unquenchable fire – there forever to –'

'Not for ever,' I exclaimed, "only till he has paid the uttermost farthing" for "If any man's work abide not the fire, he shall suffer loss, yet himself shall be saved, but so as by fire," and He that "is able to subdue all things to Himself, will have all men to be saved," and "will in the fulness of time, gather together in one all things in Christ Jesus, who tasted death for every man, and in whom God will reconcile all things to himself, whether they be things in earth or things in heaven."'

'Oh, Helen! where did you learn all this?'

'In the Bible, aunt. I have searched it through, and found nearly thirty passages, all tending to support the same theory.'

'And is *that* the use you make of your Bible? And did you find no passages tending to prove the danger and falsity of such a belief?'

'No: I found, indeed, some passages that, taken by themselves, might seem to contradict that opinion; but they will all bear a different construction to that which is commonly given, and in most the only difficulty is in the word which we translate "everlasting" or "eternal". I don't know the Greek, but I believe it strictly means for ages, and might signify either "endless" or "long-enduring". And as for the danger of the belief, I would not publish it abroad, if I thought any poor wretch would be likely to presume upon it to his own destruction, but it

> is a glorious thought to cherish in one's own heart, and I would not part with it for all the world can give!'[20]

Stevie Davies highlights the point at which Helen disagrees with her aunt that she and Arthur will be separated forever:

> *Not for ever*: this phrase is the important pivot upon which turns Anne Brontë's version of the Brontë antagonism to the Christian vision of eternal hell as the punishment of sinners. Whereas Emily Brontë denied the goodness of God in the light of his punitive morality, Anne Brontë denied the eternity of hell as inconsistent with a loving Father: 'even the wicked shall at last / Be fitted for the skies'.[21]

It is apparent to the reader that Arthur Huntingdon is as terrible as Helen's aunt makes him out to be, and we spend the rest of the book watching Arthur devolve further into drinking and gambling, until of course Helen takes her child and leaves. It would have made sense for Helen to do a complete turn in her beliefs at this point, but when she hears that her husband is gravely ill, she doesn't abandon her hope that anyone can be saved. She returns to Arthur, confident in the belief that though he may be on his way to hell, he won't be there forever.

When Gilbert Markham learns of Helen's return to her husband, he is as shocked as the reader and immediately goes to visit Helen's brother, Frederick Lawrence, to confirm that Helen is gone.

> My companion gravely took my arm, and leading me away to the garden, thus answered my question: –
>
> 'She is at Grassdale Manor, in —shire.'

'Where?' cried I, with a convulsive start.

'At Grassdale Manor.'

'How was it?' I gasped. 'Who betrayed her?'

'She went of her own accord.'

'Impossible, Lawrence!! She *could* not be so frantic!' exclaimed I, vehemently grasping his arm, as if to force him to unsay those hateful words.

'She did,' persisted he in the same grave, collected manner as before – 'and not without reason,' he continued, gently disengaging himself from my grasp: 'Mr Huntingdon is ill.'

'And so she went to nurse him?'

'Yes.'

'Fool!' I could not help exclaiming – and Lawrence looked up with a rather reproachful glance. 'Is he dying then?'

'I think not, Markham.'

'And how many more nurses has he? – How many ladies are there besides, to take care of him?'

'None; he was alone or she would not have gone.'

'Oh, confound it! this is intolerable!'

'What is? That he should be alone?' I attempted no reply, for I was not sure that this circumstance did not partly conduce to my distraction. I therefore continued to pace the walk in silent anguish, with my hand pressed to my forehead; then suddenly pausing and turning to my companion, I impatiently exclaimed,

'Why did she take this infatuated step? What fiend persuaded her to it?'

'Nothing persuaded her but her own sense of duty.'

'Humbug!'

'I was half inclined to say so myself, Markham, at first.

> I assure you it was not by my advice that she went, for I detest that man as fervently as you can do – except, indeed, that his reformation would give me much greater pleasure than his death: – but all I did was to inform her of the circumstance of his illness (the consequence of a fall from his horse in hunting), and to tell her that that unhappy person, Miss Myers, had left him some time ago.'
>
> 'It was ill done! Now, when he finds the convenience of her presence, he will make all manner of lying speeches and false, fair promises for the future, and she will believe him, and then her condition will be ten times worse and ten times more irremediable than before.'[22]

Both men are upset that she has returned, Gilbert even assuming that someone must have betrayed Helen's whereabouts to Arthur. He finds it impossible that she should return to him by her own choice, and her brother Frederick assures Gilbert that he advised her against returning. It is clear that neither of them likes the idea, and Gilbert especially thinks it foolish.

A note here on Anne's humour: Frederick does not immediately give Gilbert all the information that he has. He lets Gilbert stew, pace around the garden, curse and be outraged before he tries to soothe his mind. The two characters have a fairly fraught relationship, and Frederick is not completely sold on the idea of having Gilbert as a brother-in-law. He subtly implies that he knows, too, that Gilbert probably welcomes Arthur's death, as much for selfish reasons as for Helen's safety and freedom. So even in a scene of high tension, Gilbert and Frederick remain 'in character'. Anne's perception when it comes to human psychology, and her skill as a writer, add depth to this scene: on the surface we have Gilbert asking where Helen is; just underneath, we have the tension between Gilbert and Helen's brother. Once

Gilbert is done being dramatic, Frederick tells him that there is less to worry about than he thinks, and hands him a letter from Helen that he has had the whole time they have been conversing.

It is clear that Helen holds more power this time than she did when she lived with Arthur as his new wife. The letters to her brother portray a confidence that her diary did not – she is ultimately in charge of her fate. Helen left in the first place to save her son from the influence of her husband and his friends. She returns out of a sense of duty as his wife, and to save her husband – as she would for any human being that she knew to be suffering.

I believe that Anne made Helen feel drawn towards the concepts of Universal Salvation in the same way that she was drawn to them. I have always interpreted Anne to be someone who had a lot of empathy for others, who was very compassionate, and as someone who seriously tried to understand the motivations of others. Helen also feels empathy and compassion for others, so it would be very out of character for her to ignore the suffering of a fellow human, even one that had wronged her in the past. It naturally follows that this sensitivity and kind-heartedness led Anne – and therefore Helen – to find the concepts of Universal Salvation in their own Bibles.

Helen's time with the sick Arthur is recorded in letters that she writes to Frederick. She writes of Arthur's mental torment and his fear of death. He begins to find a new affection for Helen, as the only one that can save him and the only one attempting to give him any comfort. Helen tries her best to assure him that if he repents, he will find himself in heaven when he dies, but Arthur's fear of hell and eternal punishment makes him switch dramatically between beginning to entertain hope, and plunging back into complete denial. A conversation between Arthur and Helen begins like this:

> 'I can't repent, I only fear.'
>
> 'You only regret the past for its consequences to yourself?'
>
> 'Just so – except that I'm sorry to have wronged you Nell, because you're so good to me.'
>
> 'Think of the goodness of God, and you cannot but be grieved to have offended Him?'
>
> 'What *is* God – I cannot see Him or hear Him? – God is only an idea.'[23]

Here, Arthur is very clearly taking an atheist stance and asserting that he cannot repent. The conversation quickly switches to Arthur asking again for Helen's help, however. She tries her best to comfort someone who is scared to believe in God because of what that belief might mean for them. Helen is aware that Arthur's atheism, unlike modern atheism, is fuelled by the fear of eternal punishment. She offers him the ideas of Universal Salvation, but Arthur clearly knows that he has acted terribly throughout his life, and so clings to Helen in his dying moments. Her final letter to her brother is again filled with her characteristic compassion and hope, echoing the words she said to her aunt when she first talked to her about her theological beliefs:

> 'Oh Frederick! none can imagine the miseries, bodily and mental, of that death bed! How could I endure to think that that poor trembling soul was hired away to everlasting torment? it would drive me mad! But thank God I have hope – not only from a vague dependence on the possibility that penitence and pardon might have reached him at last, but from the blessed confidence that, through whatever purging fires the erring spirit may be doomed to pass – whatever fate awaits it, still, it is not

> lost, and God, who hatter nothing that he hath made, *will* bless it in the end!'[24]

At this point, with Arthur out of the way, the modern reader may simply be happy that the path is now clear for Helen and Gilbert to marry. Arthur had not allowed Helen to separate from him, meaning that there was no way that Helen could have fought for a legal separation. Arthur's death, therefore, was the only way in which Helen could fully regain control over her own life and that of her son. His death is a relief, one that even Gilbert had hoped for, despite knowing it is wrong to wish death upon someone.

People who read the book when it came out, however, would have been shocked, or at least made uncomfortable, by the deathbed conversations recorded by Helen. Firstly, there are Arthur's atheistic views – to be an atheist at that time was even more controversial than to be a Dissenter. In Victorian Britain, anyone who refused to swear to Christian oaths was unable to give evidence in court, for example. Percy Bysshe Shelley, a favourite of Branwell especially, was expelled from Oxford University after publishing a pamphlet entitled *The Necessity of Atheism*. He was also denied custody of his children partially because he was an atheist.

Secondly, there were Anne's views on Universal Salvation. She was well aware that Universal Salvation was a controversial topic within the Anglican Church, which is why Helen never explicitly states that she believes in it. Instead, Anne disguised the doctrine of Universal Salvation as Helen's own personal interpretation of the Bible, and has her practise her belief when she returns to her dying husband. This approach did not fool some of the critics, and *Sharpe's London Magazine* wrote about the foolishness of believing in such a doctrine, saying that it 'becomes scarcely necessary, in order to convince our readers of the madness of trusting to such a forced distortion of the Divine attribute of mercy, to add that this doctrine is alike repugnant to Scripture, and in direct opposition to the teaching of the Anglican Church.'[25]

Anne did at least gain some approval. It came from the Reverend David Thom of Liverpool, who sent 'an enthusiastic and flattering' letter, 'congratulating her on her espousal of the doctrine of Universal Salvation in *The Tenant of Wildfell Hall*.'[26] Anne wrote back to him, grateful to have found someone else who shared her beliefs and expressing how deeply her religious ideas ran through everything that she did: 'I have cherished [Universal Salvation] from my very childhood – with a trembling hope at first, and afterwards with a firm and glad conviction of its truth.'[27]

Percy Bysshe Shelley: he wrote a pamphlet 'The Necessity of Atheism'.

Anne used Helen's story in *Wildfell Hall* as a way to share her own religious beliefs in a way that would have been more acceptable, and also more entertaining, than to simply write a religious pamphlet or straightforward moralistic tale. By writing about religion and theological issues in this way, Anne was stepping into the patriarchal territory of the clergy. This was something that she had also done with *Agnes Grey*, in which she criticises the sermon style of the character Mr Hatfield, while celebrating the conduct, sermons and advice given by the parson Edward Weston.

As a member of the clergy himself, Anne's father had written two religious stories, and several of his sermons were published (including the one he gave at the funeral of his curate William Weightman). The idea of the published sermon or the moralistic pamphlet was therefore not unknown to Anne. There was also Anne's 'Bible Project', which saw her make notes and highlight important passages in her Bible. All these influences, coupled with a thoughtful and analytical mind, helped to produce *Agnes Grey* and *Wildfell Hall*.

Agnes Grey is littered throughout with appraisals of the clergy. This is most obvious in Chapter 11, 'The Cottagers', when Nancy Brown tells Agnes about her religious crisis (a crisis that was very similar to the one Anne experienced at Roe Head). Nancy asks the Reverend Hatfield for some advice, but his response is not particularly helpful:

> '[…] he like seemed to scorn me. I might be mista'en – but he like gave a sort of a whistle, and I saw a bit of a smile on his face; and he said "Oh it's all stuff! You've been among the Methodists, my good woman." But I telled him I'd never been near the Methodies/ And then he said, –

> "'Well,' says he, 'you must come to church, where you'll hear the Scriptures properly explained, instead of sitting poring over your Bible at home.'"[28]

Anne herself was guilty of 'poring over [her] Bible at home' and knew just how much of a beneficial exercise it could be. She and her siblings valued the personal interpretations that could be gained by studying the Bible for themselves, and all were against the idea that being a Christian just meant attendance at church and relying on the clergy to provide them with interpretations and instructions for worship. This, therefore, was Anne's first criticism against Mr Hatfield (and others like him): their refusal to engage with their parishioners and encourage them to study by themselves outside of church. His word goes, and if Nancy went to church, she would know that.

Nancy, however, complains that she cannot make it to church because of ill health, but Mr Hatfield simply says that she can't use not being able to walk as an excuse. Nancy responds with an argument that Anne was very passionate about herself:

> 'But please, sir,' says I, 'if I do go to church, what the better shall I be? I want to have my sins blotted out, and to feel that they are remembered no more against me, and that the love of God is shed abroad in my heart; and if I can get no good by reading my Bible an' saying my prayers at him, what good shall I get by going to church?'[29]

Mr Hatfield once more refuses to be sympathetic to Nancy's troubles and tells her that going to church should fix her. And if it doesn't, then she must be one of those lazy people who wants to get into heaven by doing the least amount of work possible. The irony here i that Mr Hatfield is the one doing the least amount of work – as a man of the church, he should be doing everything he can to help his parishioners through times of trouble. Nancy is the one doing the work – reading her Bible at home when she can't get to church, and confiding in Mr Hatfield – and after speaking to him she agrees to make a greater effort to go to church.

But, because she is only doing it because she has been told to, simply going to church is not enough: it felt like '"a sore labour an' a heavy task beside, instead of a blessing and a privilege as all good Christians does. It seemed like as all were barren an' dark to me."'[30] One day, after church, Nancy again approaches Mr Hatfield, only to hear him refer to her as 'a canting old fool!' to Mr Weston; the term 'canting' was derogatory slang for someone who had been studying Methodist doctrine. Mr Weston, the better example of what a clergyman should be, then visits Nancy Brown. He invites her to tell him all her problems, and listens, and gives her the advice that Mr Hatfield wouldn't (or more likely couldn't) give to her.

Mr Weston takes complicated parts of Scripture and makes them easier to understand, in a way that Mr Hatfield, with his boring sermons and his scorning ways, cannot. He tells her that going to church is not the entirety of a Christian's duty, but they must take what they learn in church and practice it outside. He urges her that she must learn to love and be kind to her neighbours, even though they vex her. In short, the qualities that Mr Weston possesses are far superior to those of Mr Hatfield (he is even nice to Nancy's cat; Mr Hatfield, in comparison, kicked it) and so Mr Weston is better at his job.

In an essay titled 'Preaching to the clergy', Jennifer M. Stolpa argues that *Agnes Grey* was Anne's attempt at showing what an ideal sermon should look like. Anne does this by contrasting Weston and Hatfield's sermon styles:

Weston's sermon 'clearly developed the [biblical] text he chose and focused on its applications to daily life'; Hatfield's treated 'the biblical text with less reverence and care' and 'the language indicates that his own composition is treated as more important than the biblical text'.[31]

In expressing her views on sermon styles and criticising the approach of some members of the clergy, Anne was completely ignoring the advice of the prominent Victorian thinker John Ruskin, who asserted that theology was 'one dangerous science for women'.[32] In *Agnes Grey*, Anne managed to write about her criticisms of organised religion and frame it as a character study of two men. It sets Mr Weston up as the more desirable of the two, and serves as a way of increasing Agnes's interest in him. As she did with Universal Salvation in *Wildfell Hall*, Anne disguised the issues she wanted to write about so that readers would only be able to recognise what she was trying to do if they knew what to look for. Otherwise you wouldn't notice and would simply enjoy an excellent book. It's a mark of her skill as a writer that she was able to get these fairly heavy issues into the novel and still make it interesting to read.

* * *

In her 'Biographical Notice', Charlotte suggests that Anne did not enjoy the process of writing *The Tenant of Wildfell Hall*. She paints a picture of an Anne who felt compelled by religious duty to record in full the 'terrible effects of talents misused and faculties abused' – the unfortunate decline of capable people due to addiction and societal expectation.[33] Charlotte states plainly that 'she hated her work' as if this was a fact, but reading Anne's work gives a completely different view. It's clear that Anne was passionate about her faith, and the way in which she interpreted the Bible. She wanted people to be able to engage with her beliefs and used her talents as a writer to do so. Anne achieved something that is very difficult to pull off well: she wrote about big ideas and important issues in a way that was entertaining and subtle. She created characters and scenarios that were strong enough to hold up the themes and beliefs that she was trying to communicate.

A possible contemporary equivalent to Anne is Sufjan Stevens, a musician whose own religious melancholy inspires his bittersweet indie pop music. He turns sermons into relatable lyrics and does it so well that you don't even notice his Christianity until you start to pay attention to the lyrics. There's honesty in Anne's painful, sad poetry that reflects many readers' own experiences too, not just those readers who are also religious. And neither Anne nor Sufjan Stevens writes to be sad or shocking purely for the sake of it – their art wouldn't be as powerful if that was the case. There's generally a feeling of disgust or distaste when it's obvious that a writer or artist is exploiting sad situations to manipulate people. With Anne's work, there is often disgust, but never with the text itself – it's a reaction to the characters she has built so well. Many artists and writers put their faith at the centre of their works, as Anne does, which makes it all the more astonishing that Anne is often dismissed for being too religious, or too preachy.

Anne made use of her sense of humour, too. Whether she did it on purpose or not, both *Agnes Grey* and *Wildfell Hall* are, in parts, very funny – Gilbert's younger brother comes to mind, an immediately identifiable teenage brother with plenty of annoying and obnoxious things to say to his siblings. Agnes's dry wit when observing people doesn't feel like it was the kind of thing that an author would write out of a sense of duty. The subject matter of *Wildfell Hall* may be heavy, but it doesn't suffer from the stiltedness you would expect from an author who hated her work. She was pious, and she studied her Bible diligently. But the way she was taught to think about her Bible was not the way that she interpreted it for herself. Where others saw predetermined sin and damnation, she saw love and forgiveness. She believed that anyone could be saved and thought that was a message worth sharing.

Anne's desire to improve herself, her ability to see the best in others, and her constant hard work to make the lives of others better were the main things that stood out to me when I learned more about her religious views. Her belief in Universal Salvation and her dedication to her 'Bible Project' were at the back of my mind when I watched the American sitcom *The Good Place*, which focuses on a group of friends who are trying to prove that anyone can become a good person, even after they're dead. Anne believed that people *could* and *did* become better people, that everyone would eventually make it into her version of the 'Good Place': heaven. The show even deals with some of the things that Anne was interested in herself: does being an authority figure with influence automatically make you a good person? Does knowing all the rules make you a good person? Anne, much like the characters in *The Good Place*, realised early that the way you treat others and approach obstacles is a much better measure of how good a person is. And even then, you can always do better.

SIX

ANNE'S SOCIAL CONSCIENCE

Anne's final letter to Ellen Nussey, written shortly before she died, gives us a brief and accurate snapshot of how Anne wished to live: she wanted 'to do some good in the world'.[1] Not only that, she wanted to make life better not just for those closest to her but for anyone she could possibly influence. Her preface to the second edition of *The Tenant of Wildfell Hall* makes it clear that telling the truth was, for her, one way of achieving that aim:

> Let it not be imagined, however, that I consider myself competent to reform the errors and abuses of society, but only that I would fain contribute my humble quota towards so good an aim, and if I can gain the public ear at all, I would rather whisper a few wholesome truths therein than whisper much soft nonsense.[2]

Anne's conscientious and thoughtful nature would have made it almost impossible for her to overlook the 'errors and abuses of society'. From a young age, the Brontës had all taken a keen interest in current affairs and politics, and they were aware that their father often campaigned for causes he was passionate about – they may even have seen his letters and articles in newspapers. In 1837, for example, Patrick was working hard to oppose the government and petition parliament to repeal the Poor Law Amendment Act of 1834. This act ended all income support for those who needed it, which resulted in a huge increase in workhouse populations. Workhouses were especially sinister because of the segregation rules they employed; sexes were separated and split into age groups. Families had to choose between starving to death and staying together, or entering the workhouse and being split up.[3] Meetings to discuss such issues often took place in the Sunday school room at Haworth.

It's no surprise, then, that the daughter of one of the most vehement opposers to this law, and others like it, would grow up to focus her talents on making the world a better place:

> [...] I love to give innocent pleasure. Yet, be it understood, I shall not limit my ambition to this, – or even to producing 'a perfect work of art': time and talents so spent, I should consider wasted and misapplied. Such humble talents as God has given me I will endeavour to put to their greatest use; if I am able to amuse I will try to benefit too; and when I feel it my duty to speak an unpalatable truth, with the help of God, I *will* speak it, though it be to the prejudice of my name and to the detriment of my reader's immediate pleasure as well as my own.[4]

Anne's works were shocking, not just because of the bad behaviour she wrote about (see Huntingdon and his companions), but because of the very specific focus that she put onto that behaviour. She shone a light on things that people didn't want to talk about or acknowledge. It was expected that women would know their place and carry out their duties to the best of their ability. But if a husband was abusive, an alcoholic, or gambled the family's fortune away, a wife had no way of legally separating herself. Anne was writing about emotional abuse and controlling behaviour almost two hundred years before laws against it were put into place in the UK.

But Anne didn't just focus on the problems within marriages and marital law; she took it further. What caused these problems in the first place? What made men think they could act in such a way, and why were women putting up with it? To find answers, she went right back to childhood. Her two novels both tackle ideas about education, how it differs for young boys and girls, and the emphasis on 'building character' that was often put on small boys. She writes about the options that were open to women at the time, and how limiting their education was. Anne's own father was an excellent example of the power of education: he had gone from living in poverty, to being sponsored through Cambridge, to being a perpetual curate with the power to change other people's lives for the better, and all because he wanted an education. Anne also knew, however, that the same options that were open to her father were not open to her simply because she was a woman.

Anne wasn't scared to be controversial when it came to her views on religion, and she wasn't afraid to write about other controversial topics that affected society. When I first started reading Anne's books, at most I was expecting some moralistic tales about being a good and pious Christian. I had no idea just how opinionated she was, or how unafraid she was to voice those opinions, no matter how contentious. And it was a revelation to read in *Agnes Grey* and *Wildfell Hall* about issues that are still relatable and relevant to today's readers.

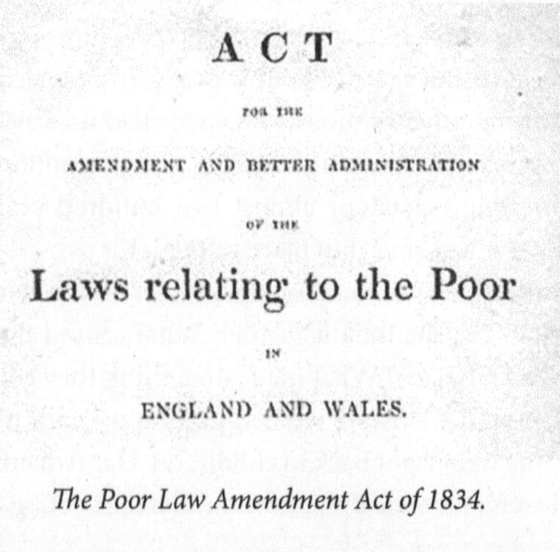
ACT

FOR THE

AMENDMENT AND BETTER ADMINISTRATION

OF THE

Laws relating to the Poor

IN

ENGLAND AND WALES.

The Poor Law Amendment Act of 1834.

ANNE AND EDUCATION

All the Brontë siblings grew up knowing that they would have to earn a living one day. The family could not survive on their father's wage alone, and there weren't any savings or an inheritance to speak of that would have let them live without having to work. To this end, Patrick made sure that his children were educated. All of his daughters spent some time in a school, and he took on the responsibility of educating Branwell himself. The girls, too, benefitted from Branwell's lessons, and were actively encouraged to join in by their father, meaning they also picked up bits and pieces of a classical education.

The value Patrick placed on education can be seen by the fact that he gave 'instructions to his children at stated times during the day, adapted to their various ages and capacities'.[5] Anne took her own formal education seriously: while at Roe Head she received an award for good conduct, and by the end of her education was able to offer all the accomplishments required of a governess: music, singing, drawing, French. She could offer Latin, geography and history, too, for which she had her father to thank. From a young age, Anne was very aware of the differences between boys' and girls' education: she had to learn how to sew, to mend and make clothes; Anne, Emily and Charlotte all knew how to bake, how to 'pilluputate' (peel a potato),[6] how to make bread. As a boy, Branwell was not expected to learn these things.

In *Agnes Grey*, Anne writes about a typical education for young women, and the effect that it has on her pupils, Rosalie and Matilda Murray. The girls are completely different, both in appearance and temperament: Rosalie is the most conventionally pretty of the two; Matilda 'might possibly make a handsome woman, but she was far too big-boned and awkward to ever be a pretty girl, and, at present, she cared little about it'.[7]

Rosalie is spoiled, selfish, accustomed to being indulged and lacks empathy. Agnes, however, grows to like her, 'not only because she had taken a fancy to me, but because there was so much of what was pleasing and pre-possessing in herself'.[8] Agnes attributes Rosalie's failings (as she sees them) to the upbringing of all of the Murray children: 'She had never been properly taught the distinction between right and wrong; she had, like her brothers and sisters, been suffered from infancy to tyrannise over nurses, governesses, and servants.'[9] This is as much a criticism of the attitudes of wealthy parents towards their children as it is a criticism of the education women were expected to receive, and she later expresses her sadness that even the young boys of the family are ignorant of most of their lessons.

When it comes to illustrating the importance of education for girls, Anne hits the nail on the head by describing Rosalie's (lack of) interest in her lessons: 'Her mind had never been cultivated: her intellect at best was somewhat shallow; she possessed considerable vivacity, some quickness of perception, and some talent for music and the acquisition of languages, but till fifteen she had troubled herself to acquire nothing; – then the love of display had roused her faculties, and induced her to apply herself, but only to the more showy accomplishments [...] everything was neglected but French, German, music, singing, dancing, fancy-work, and a little drawing.'[10] Rosalie is bright and intelligent, and with some encouragement, could achieve much more than just the 'showy accomplishments', in Agnes's opinion.

It is utterly tragic that Rosalie's self-worth is completely determined by how much attention she can get by displaying her singing and dancing abilities, or by speaking a few lines in French or German. As an upper-class lady, Rosalie would have been expected to marry, and to make a good match, which meant attracting a rich husband. I find it especially unsettling to imagine young girls performing what they have learned, almost as if showing off to a teacher, in an attempt to draw the attention of a man. It firmly places the men as authority figures, capable of assessing a lady's worth based purely on her looks and those 'showy accomplishments'. It's especially sad knowing that, if she had been so encouraged, Rosalie could have achieved so much more. Not only that, but her sense of self-worth would have been much higher, possibly allowing her to go against her mother's wishes and choose a husband for herself, one she could respect (or no husband at all).

Anne was not the first to point out this failure of the country's young women at the time. Fifty years before the publication of *Agnes Grey*, in 1792, Mary Wollstonecraft had published *A Vindication of the Rights of Woman*, in which she argued that serious thought had to be put into women's education, if they were to be taken seriously. How could they be expected to be men's intellectual equal if they weren't offered the same opportunities in terms of cultivation of the mind?

Many advice manuals on the education of women were circulating during Wollstonecraft's time, a lot of them even written by women. They were incredibly patronising and went against everything that Wollstonecraft and, later, Anne, believed in: 'The poet Anne Barbauld, herself an accomplished writer and schoolmistress, declared girls too "delicate" to be independent from men, even as she took care of her mentally ill husband and was her family's sole provider. For Barbauld, females were created "for pleasure and delight alone," and, therefore, teachers should focus on teaching girls how to please. […] Hannah More believed that parents and teachers should drive the "bold, independent, enterprising spirit" out of girls while nurturing it in boys.'[11]

Wollstonecraft wrote in her *Vindication* that 'To render women truly useful members of society, I argue that they should be led, by having their understandings cultivated on a large scale, to acquire a rational affection for their country, founded on knowledge, because it is obvious that we are little interested about what we do not understand.'[12] Perhaps Rosalie Murray would have made better use of her intellect, and the talents she possessed, if someone had given her a reason to do so. Unfortunately for the Murray girls, their mother was more in accordance with the ideas of Anne Barbauld and Hannah Moore than she was with Mary Wollestoncraft and Anne Brontë.

I always feel sorry for Matilda whenever I read *Agnes Grey* – not being graceful and 'positively beautiful' like her sister, she is possibly aware that her options are limited when it comes to finding a husband. The idea of marriage doesn't particularly interest her, and so she is aimless, on the periphery of things. Even Agnes is not especially sympathetic towards her, but Anne's choice to include such a character serves to illustrate what sometimes happened to young girls who felt ostracised by societal expectations. 'Matilda thought she was well enough, but cared little about the matter; still less did she care about the cultivation of her mind and the acquisition of ornamental accomplishments.'[13] As far as Matilda was concerned, a governess was only good for teaching those things that would help her to get the attention of a future husband. Like Rosalie, if she had been shown some other purpose for attaining an education, she may have shown more interest.

As soon as Matilda leaves the school room, however, 'her ill-humour was generally over too; while riding her spirited pony, or romping with the dogs or her brothers and sister, but especially with her dear brother John, she was as happy as a lark.'[14] Matilda clearly had interests, which mostly involved being outdoors, and it's depressing to think that there were other girls like her who were never encouraged to pursue their own paths in life. 'Her mother was partly aware of her deficiencies, and gave me many a lecture as to how I should try to form her tastes, and endeavour to rouse and cherish her dormant vanity.'[15] Even Matilda's mother only wanted her daughter to crave attention; she didn't care that Matilda might have other interests.

In one of my favourite passages in *Wildfell Hall*, Helen Graham expresses her views to a shocked and disapproving company about the double standards present in the belief that boys and girls should be educated differently according to their gender:

> 'You would have us encourage our sons to prove all things by their own experience, while our daughters must not even profit by the experience of others. Now *I* would have both so to benefit by the experience of others, and the precepts of a higher authority, that they should know beforehand to refuse the evil and choose the good, and require no experimental proofs to teach them the evil of transgression. I would not send a poor girl into the world, unarmed against her foes, and ignorant of the snares that beset her path; nor would I watch and guard her, till, deprived of self-respect and self-reliance, she lost the power, or the will, to watch and guard herself; – and as for my son – if I thought he would grow up to be what you call a man of the world – one that has "*seen life*," and glories in his experience, even though he should so far profit by it, as to sober down, at length, into a useful and respected member of society – I would rather that he died tomorrow! – rather a thousand times!!'[16]

Anne reiterates and expands on what she first wrote about in *Agnes Grey*: that to deprive girls of an education, to guard them so closely that they lose their self-respect, will ultimately remove any awareness of themselves as anything other than subservient to their future husbands or the other men in their lives. It removes their autonomy, while at the same time encouraging boys that they should throw themselves into the world, and at vices, to build up their character. Anne, like Mary Wollstonecraft, believed that in failing women and girls, society was failing everybody. Men and young boys also suffered from the attitude that women were meant to be subservient, that their lessons should be focused on pleasing men.

Anne didn't only write about the shortcomings of girls' education – she had a lot to say about the way boys were educated too. And it's also an issue that still exercises us in the twenty-first century. In January 2019, the men's razor firm Gillette released an advert that caused a huge amount of controversy. The advert featured scenes of sexual harassment, bullying and fighting, and invited viewers to re-think the behaviour they were portraying. The line 'boys will be boys' was questioned as a valid excuse for the behaviour shown in the clip, and instead, viewers were encouraged to challenge themselves to do more, to be better version of themselves, and to set a better example for the next generation of men.

The advert received more than its fair share of backlash – Gillette was accused of alienating its target demographic and pandering to feminists. But there was a lot of positive feedback, too, with people congratulating the brand on the changes they have been making regarding how they advertise themselves. The president of Gillette told the BBC, 'Effective immediately, [we] will review all public-facing content against a set of defined standards meant to ensure we fully reflect the ideals of

Respect, Accountability and Role Modelling in the ads we run, the images we publish to social media, the words we choose, and more. For us, the decision to publicly assert our beliefs while celebrating men who are doing things right was an easy choice that makes a difference.'[17]

Anne Brontë wrote about these ideas in *Wildfell Hall* almost two centuries ago. When Helen tells Mrs Markham that she refuses to let her son drink alcohol, Mrs Markham responds with shock: '"I really gave you credit for having more sense – The poor child will be the veriest milksop that ever was sopped! Only think what a man you will make of him, if you persist."' Gilbert Markham then tries to argue that the only way boys grow up to be virtuous men is to go it alone, and learn to walk over those obstacles that present themselves. '"What is it that constitutes virtue, Mrs Graham?"' he asks, '"Is it the circumstance of being able and willing to resist temptations; or that of having no temptations to resist?"'[18]

Helen argues that in helping to show her son the way, she is not spoiling him; she is educating him about how to navigate the world, as any loving parent should. She makes the point that young girls are not expected to go out into the world alone, so why should boys be expected to do so? Is it because girls are less likely to resist temptation? Or is it that girls will be ruined, while boys will be strengthened by the experience? And why should there be a distinction between the two in the first place? She leaves the family very much perplexed, especially Gilbert, who doesn't fully agree with Helen, though he recognises that in his position as the eldest son he has been spoiled somewhat.

Prior to meeting Gilbert and his family, Helen had married Arthur Huntingdon, an extreme example of how a man's character was ruined by the societal expectation that men should be deferred to, allowed to have their own way, and become 'men of the world'. As a full grown man, his behaviour is like that of a child, and his influence on Helen's young son is what finally makes Helen decide that she has to leave: 'My greatest source of uneasiness, in this time of trial, was my son, whom his father and his father's friends delighted to encourage in all the embryo vices a little child can show, and to instruct in all the evil habits he could acquire – in a word, to "make a man of him" was one of their staple amusements.'[19] It pains Helen to see her young son 'tipple wine like papa' and 'swear like Mr Hattersley', while asking his mother why she never smiles. She decides to remove her son before he learns to disdain her, as young boys were taught to have less respect for the women in their lives.

In *Agnes Grey*, the character of Uncle Robson is described as 'the scorner of the female sex'. He is the favourite uncle of the Bloomfield children, and Agnes particularly despairs of his visits and his influence:

> He seldom deigned to notice me; and when he did, it was with a certain supercilious insolence of tone and manner that convinced me that he was no gentleman, though it was intended to have a contrary effect. But it was not for that I disliked his coming, so much as for the harm he did the children – encouraging all their evil propensities, and undoing, in a few minutes, the little good it had taken me months of labour to achieve.[20]

He ignored the youngest children, but Mary Ann was a particular favourite, and he constantly complimented her looks and 'was continually encouraging her tendency to affectation'.[21] Uncle Robson is the one who gives Agnes's pupil Tom a birds' nest, which Agnes crushes before Tom can torture the poor chicks. Tom runs to his uncle, who laughs as Tom shouts and insults Agnes. Uncle Robson promises to bring Tom a new nest the next day, while singing his praises: '"Damme, but the lad has some spunk in him too. Curse me, if ever I saw a nobler little scoundrel than that. He's beyond petticoat government already; – by G –, he defies mother, granny, governess, all!"'[22]

Uncle Robson and Arthur Huntingdon are examples of what becomes of boys who are told to disrespect women, who are taught from a young age to 'tipple wine', that to terrorise animals shows spunk and is demonstrative of manly behaviour – they become despised by the women around them. These are the women who teach them, who cook for them, who put their well-being above their own.

In his book *How Not To Be A Boy*, the comic actor Robert Webb writes about how the expectations placed on men, which haven't changed much since Anne's time, are detrimental to everyone, and especially to men's mental health. The cover of the book has the 'rules for being a man' written in capitals, and they're rules that could easily have been given by Mrs Markham to Helen to 'help' her to raise her son: 'DON'T CRY, LOVE SPORTS, PLAY ROUGH, DRINK BEER, DON'T TALK ABOUT FEELINGS.'[23]

Anne's novels are full of male characters that, because of the way society expected boys to be brought up, are now repellent to most of the women in their lives. Their lack of emotional intelligence results in the kind of spoilt behaviour that, in the case of Arthur Huntingdon, leads to his eventual downfall. There are characters, like Lowborough, who are capable of reform. There are even men, like Mr Weston, who show that it's possible to be good in a climate that expects men in positions of power to look out only for themselves. Ultimately, Anne wanted to draw attention to the power of education, and how a good education for both girls and boys can go a long way towards building equality – we don't have to tell boys that they need to be manly, play rough and disrespect women, and the world would be a better place if we didn't.

OPPORTUNITIES FOR WOMEN

In both *Agnes Grey* and *Wildfell Hall* Anne poses the question: what are bright, intelligent women supposed to do with their lives? What should they aim for? Agnes, unsatisfied with being the baby of the family and not being allowed to contribute in any meaningful way, finds employment as a governess in two separate posts. In *Wildfell Hall*, Anne explores how encouraging the idea of marriage as the ultimate goal can have disastrous consequences, and how teaching girls that to be admired is more important than anything else can result in characters like Annabella Wilmot, Rosalie Murray and Eliza Millward. Annabella Wilmot secured a title when she married Lord Lowborough, and then continued to chase attention when she had an affair with Helen's husband. Rosalie Murray and Eliza Millward are less sinister than Annabella, but their lack of education has wasted any talents they may have had. Both are flirts whose only pleasure lies in attracting attention.

Anne, who had grown up in a loving family with access to a more masculine education than most, was aware that she would need to work for a living and prepared herself to the best of her abilities. She carried her values into her work as a governess, and later into her novels. She was also aware that opportunities for upper- and middle-class women were very limited: they could get married, be resigned to spinsterhood, or they could go to work as a teacher, either as a governess or in a school for girls. Always, though, women were to be in servitude to men – either from their employers, or the men in their personal lives.

In *Wildfell Hall*, Anne expresses her frustration at this subservience through Gilbert Markham's younger sister, Rose. When Gilbert comes in unexpectedly late one evening, his mother scolds him a little but proceeds to lay out the meal that he missed and which she has kept warm. Gilbert complains that the tea is not fresh, and his mother immediately instructs Rose to make him some more. Rose makes it known that she is not happy with the events.

> 'Well! — if it had been *me* now, I should have had no tea at all — If it had been Fergus, even, he would have had to put up with such as there was, and been told to be thankful, for it was far too good for him; but *you* — we can't do too much for you — It's always so — if there's anything particularly nice at table, Mamma winks and nods at me, to abstain from it, and if I don't attend to that, she whispers "Don't eat so much of that, Rose, Gilbert will like it for his supper" — *I'm* nothing at all — in the parlour, it's "Come Rose, put away your things, and let's have the room nice and tidy against they come in; and keep up a good fire; Gilbert likes a cheerful fire." In the kitchen — "Make that pie a large one, Rose, I dare say the boys'll be hungry; — and don't put so much pepper in, they'll not like it I'm sure" — or, "Rose, don't put so many spices in the pudding, Gilbert likes it plain" — or, "Mind you put plenty of currants in the cake, Fergus likes plenty." If I say, "Well Mamma, *I* don't," I'm told I ought not to think of myself — "You know Rose, in all household matters, we have only two things to consider, first, what's proper to be done, and secondly, what's most agreeable to the gentlemen of the house — anything will do for the ladies."'

> 'And very good doctrine too,' said my mother. 'Gilbert thinks so, I'm sure.'[24]

It would be nice to think that this attitude has, for the most part, disappeared. I remember that it was definitely the case for one set of grandparents, but not the other. It's something that we see less of, that women must make things 'agreeable to the gentlemen of the house'. But it does still exist. In *We Should All Be Feminists*, Nigerian writer Chimamanda Ngozi Adichie writes about a family where the daughter must cook noodles for the son, despite being just as academically gifted as him. It's a situation that is very similar to that of Rose and her brothers. Adichie goes on, 'What if the parents, from the beginning, taught *both* children to cook [noodles]? Cooking, by the way, is a useful and practical life skill for a boy to have. I've never thought it made much sense to leave such a crucial thing – the ability to nourish oneself – in the hands of others.'[25]

At least Gilbert shows the beginnings of realisation on this point, even saying that his mother's doctrine is only convenient for himself (and his brother), though it does him no good in the long run: '"I might sink into the grossest condition of self-indulgence and carelessness about the wants of others, from the mere habit of being constantly cared for myself, and having all my wants anticipated or immediately supplied, while left in total ignorance of what is done for me."'[26]

The argument continues, with Gilbert's mother telling him that he will never know how much his mother does for him until he is married, and his new wife isn't able or is unwilling to dote on him as much as his mother does. Gilbert tries to assert that this would be good for him, that he should find more happiness in making his wife happy than looking out simply for himself. Again, his mother tells him this is rubbish, and tells

Gilbert that marriage is not so; new wives are compliant and in good humour at first, but Gilbert will soon tire of petting his wife over time, as she becomes more and more of a trial. She concludes with this:

> 'Then, you must fall each into your proper place. You'll do your business, and she, if she's worthy of you, will do hers; but it's your business to please yourself, and hers to please you. I'm sure your poor, dear father was as good a husband as ever lived, and after the first six months or so were over, I should as soon have expected him to fly, as to put himself out of his way to pleasure me. He always said I was a good wife, and did my duty; and he always did his — bless him! — he was steady and punctual, seldom found fault without a reason, always did justice to my good dinners, and hardly ever spoiled my cookery by delay — and that's as much as any woman can expect of any man.'[27]

It's a concept that had permeated culture for years before Anne was writing about it: a submissive wife, whose duty is to facilitate the ambitions and daily activities of her husband. To anticipate his needs before he realises them, and to make it look effortless. Rose complains loudly (and rightly so) about waiting on her brothers, to which her mother responds saying that that is the way it should be. A woman's expectations of her husband are considered high, but really they are laughably low. They're the basic signs of mutual respect, not something to be praised beyond their worth.

At the time *Wildfell Hall* was published, however, Rose's opinions were not typically in line with those of the general public. How did Anne get away with writing such an unpopular opinion about women's position in the home, without sounding preachy? I think it is thanks to the fact that the whole novel is cleverly written as a letter to Rose's husband, J. Halford. The novel begins with Gilbert writing to his brother-in-law, and in that context it's easy to see Rose's rant against traditional domestic virtues as a funny anecdote about Rose's youth, written for the enjoyment of the man who is now her husband. It is an indictment on society at the time that, for Anne to have her characters and her ideas taken seriously, she had to frame the whole narrative within a letter written by a man (Anne was also trying to hide the fact that the book was written by a woman – the Brontës knew that women writers were subject to prejudice, hence the androgynous pseudonyms).

Gilbert ends this chapter of the letter with a question for Halford: 'Is it so Halford? Is that the extent of *your* domestic virtues; and does your happy wife exact no more?'[28] It's a question that is open to interpretation by the reader; perhaps Gilbert and Halford are laughing because Rose grew out of

'The Bottle', by George Cruikshank, who illustrated many scenes for Charles Dickens. Wives had no rights at all.

those opinions and is now the model wife that her mother was training her to be. Or maybe Gilbert is being sarcastic and is fully aware that Rose never grew out of those opinions, the joke in this case being that wives shouldn't be made to expect so little of their husbands in the first place. By framing this interaction between Gilbert, Rose and their mother as an ambiguous in-joke between two men, Anne was able to discuss an issue close to her heart while making it a part of the narrative.

Today, most of us would probably like to think that our expectations of marriage have changed considerably since the time when Anne was writing. But there has been a recent increase in the number of articles about the concept of woman-as-babysitter, where it has come from, and how we can combat it as a society. At the 2019 Hay Festival, author and psychologist Paul Dolan made headlines for saying that married people are 'fucking miserable!' – with an emphasis on how married women with children are much less happy than their single, childless counterparts. Dolan focused only on married heterosexual couples, but it's pretty disheartening that there are still women who must have similar frustrations to those felt by Rose.

Helen essentially becomes a mother to Arthur, a babysitter who has to behave according to how he would want her to behave, and tiptoes around his moods. Arthur does not know how to keep himself amused:

> Arthur is getting tired – not of me I trust, but of the idle, quiet life he leads – and no wonder, for he has so few sources of amusement; he never reads anything but newspapers and sporting magazines; and when he sees me occupied with a book, he won't let me rest till I close it. [...] I do all I can to amuse him, but it is impossible to get him to feel interested in what I most like to talk

> about; while, on the other hand, he likes to talk about things that cannot interest me – or even that annoy me – and these please him the most of all; for his favourite amusement is to sit or loll beside me on the sofa and tell me stores of his former amours, always turning upon the ruin of some confiding girl or the cozening of some unsuspecting husband; and when I express my horror and indignation, he lays it all to the charge of jealousy, and laughs till the tears run down his cheeks.[29]

Helen does all she can to entertain him, to help him out of his moods, but Arthur does nothing for her in return except tell her things that he knows she will find unpleasant. Melanie Hamlett wrote an article for *Harper's Bazaar* in May 2019 which showed that these kinds of attitudes are still alive and well. She interviewed women who had all but become live-in therapists for their boyfriends. 'Women continue to bear the burden of men's emotional lives, and why wouldn't they?' she writes. 'For generations, men have been taught to reject traits like gentleness and sensitivity, leaving them without the tools to deal with internalized anger and frustration. Meanwhile, the female savior trope continues to be romanticized on the silver screen (thanks Disney!), making it seem totally normal – even ideal – to find the man within the beast.'[30]

Helen and Arthur, brought up in a society that excused a lot of the worst behaviour of men, both fell into the same traps that a lot of people still fall into today. Helen even says to her aunt, 'provided he is not incorrigible, the more I long to deliver him from his faults – to give him an opportunity of shaking off the adventitious evil got from the contact with others worse than himself'[31], playing into the idea voiced by Rosalie Murray that 'reformed rakes make the best husbands'.[32]

Arthur Huntingdon expects his wife to amuse him, and talks at her about only those things that interest him. He actively upsets her and then expects Helen to keep herself entertained while he goes away to London alone, to spend time with his unsavoury friends. Even before they are married, Helen knows that he will never be her intellectual equal, but marries him anyway, because she thinks that she can fix him. She hardly expects anything from her husband, echoing Mrs Markham's earlier sentiments about what a woman can expect from her husband. In one of the saddest passages in the book, Helen foreshadows her own future loneliness:

> I have had several sweet letters from Arthur, already. They are not long, but passing sweet, and just like himself – full of ardent affection, and playful, lively humour; but – there is always a *but* in this imperfect world – and I do wish he would *sometimes* be serious. I cannot get him to write or speak in real, solid earnest. I don't much mind it *now*; but if it always be so, what shall I do with the serious part of myself?[33]

In the nineteenth century, women like Helen were not only taught to have low expectations of marriage, but also of employment. These middle-class women – including the Brontës – knew that if they couldn't marry, then society expected them to limit their work to the domestic sphere. They were supposed to be nurturing and gentle, and so teaching was desirable where possible.[34] All the Brontës were teachers at some point – none of them particularly liked it, and Anne's *Agnes Grey* poignantly captures the loneliness felt by a governess (see Chapter Two). Governesses weren't quite servants, but they weren't entirely respected by the family, either. This made their task especially difficult – if the children saw their parents treating the governess with disregard, then surely they could too.

But Anne took her duties as governess seriously, and used it as an opportunity to try to pass on some of her values to her pupils. Mary and Elizabeth Robinson both kept in touch with Anne after she left Thorp Green, and even visited her at Haworth in December 1848. Charlotte wrote to Ellen that 'they seemed overjoyed to see Anne; when I went into the room they were clinging around her like two children.'[35] Mary, the eldest, was at that time married to Henry Clapham of Keighley, at the desire of her mother. It is nice to imagine that Anne was able to offer advice to the two girls where their mother failed to do so (much in the same way as Rosalie and Matilda's mother did in *Agnes Grey*), consoling Mary on her poor marriage, and advising Elizabeth on how best to avoid the same fate.

Anne built up a similar relationship between Agnes and her eldest pupil Rosalie in *Agnes Grey*. After Rosalie is married, she invites Agnes to visit her in her new home, and greets her as a friend. It's clear to Agnes that Rosalie has changed, and it becomes apparent that she is unhappy in her marriage: the stately home and the rich husband she once dreamed of possessing don't make up for the fact that her husband is a drunk, with an overbearing mother. Agnes asserts that Rosalie surely knew what kind of man he was. Rosalie says that she only thought she knew: '"I did not half know him really. I know you warned me against it; and I wish I had listened to you – but it's too late to regret that now."'[36]

Many years later, after the death of her first husband, Mary Robinson married a clergyman, the Reverend George Hume Innes Pocock, vicar of Pentrich, Derbyshire. His parishioners remembered him fondly, and it's possibly thanks to Anne's influence that Mary made a much more desirable match in her second marriage.[37] Anne used every opportunity she had to teach people, and this relationship she had with her former pupils is another thing that she had in common with Mary Wollstonecraft. She also acted as a governess who often had to step in where the parents neglected or ignored their children. One of her pupils, Margaret Kingsborough, even began to rebel against her parents after being affectionately attached to Wollstonecraft. She demanded an education and refused to make a society marriage.[38] When it came to influencing young women and being a positive role model, Anne Brontë was in good company.

Some middle-class women were able to push their opportunities a little further, as Anne and her sisters did when they became writers. They were very careful to hide their identities, however, as they were aware that women writers would be met with prejudice, as Charlotte made clear in her 'Biographical Notice':

> Averse to personal publicity, we veiled our own names under those of Currer, Ellis, and Acton Bell; the ambiguous choice being dictated by a sort of conscientious scruple at assuming Christian names positively masculine, while we did not like to declare ourselves women, because – without at that time suspecting that our mode of writing and thinking was not what is called 'feminine' – we had a vague impression that authoresses are liable to be looked on with prejudice; we had noticed how critics sometimes use for their chastisement the weapon of personality, and for their reward, a flattery, which is not true praise.[39]

They knew that if their works were not feminine enough, they were likely to receive personal attacks against their character based on their choices of subjects. They also knew that if their works were good, they would be judged as good *despite* the fact that they were women; they may be patronisingly congratulated on a job well done. They didn't want any of that – they wanted to be judged on their work alone, and the only way for them to achieve that was to assume ambiguous pseudonyms.

This didn't entirely work: the Bells were criticised for their crudeness and vulgarity anyway; their works were distasteful regardless of the gender of the authors. Speculation over the genders of the Bell 'brothers' was rife, too. The details of life as a governess depicted in both *Jane Eyre* and *Agnes Grey* were too accurate for them to have been written by men. The plight of Helen Graham aroused suspicion, too, even with Anne's careful use of Gilbert as the eyes through which we see Helen for most of the novel. Not only were the authors' true genders in question, but many people believed that Currer, Ellis and Acton Bell were the same person.

Anne addressed these speculations in her preface to the second edition of *Wildfell Hall*. Not only did she use the preface to explain that even the most unbelievable aspects of the novel were true, and explain her motivations for telling such unpalatable truths, but she also used it to try and shut down the need for a clarification of the author's gender. The emphasis in the following is my own, not Anne's:

> I would have it to be distinctly understood that Acton Bell is neither Currer nor Ellis Bell, and therefore, let not his faults be attributed to them. As to whether the name be real or fictitious, it cannot greatly signify to those who know him only by his works. As little, I should think, can it matter whether the writer so designated is a man, or a woman as one or two of my critics profess to have

> discovered. I take the imputation in good part, as a compliment to the just delineation of my female characters; and though I am bound to attribute much of the severity of my censors to this suspicion, I make no effort to refute it, because, in my own mind, *I am satisfied that if a book is a good one, it is so whatever the sex of the author may be.* All novels are or should be written for both men and women to read, and I am at a loss to conceive how a man should permit himself to write anything that would be really disgraceful to a woman, or why a woman should be censured for writing anything that would be proper and becoming for a man.[40]

Anne's assertion that a book written by a woman should be just as good as a book written by a man, in fact her whole preface, was an incredibly bold move to make at that time. If it hadn't been obvious before, then the preface certainly made it clear that one of the biggest themes of *Wildfell Hall* was gender equality.

Since reading Anne's books for the first time, I have felt that Anne was more comfortable with her gender than either of her sisters. Instead of asserting herself to be Acton Bell, Anne said that her gender shouldn't matter – whereas Charlotte continued to publish as Currer Bell even after she was no longer anonymous. Anne was more than happy to be seen as a woman, as long as critics acknowledged that the work of a woman could be as good as that of a man. Even Gondal, the imaginary world she constructed with Emily, was full of women in power, compared to the damsels in distress present in Charlotte and Branwell's Angria. Not only did Agnes make it clear that even women wish for intelligent and stimulating conversation, but characters like Rose railed against the inequalities that they witnessed within the home.

Anne, like Wollstonecraft before her, believed that women were intellectually equal to men. She also believed that men were capable of emotional intelligence and of change, which is what we witness in Gilbert Markham over the course of *Wildfell Hall*. Helen's comments about raising boys strike a chord with him – he realises that he too is a spoilt son. Rose's complaints make him realise just how much his mother does for him, while making him think critically about what a woman can expect from her husband, and what she should expect. At the end of the novel he is proposed to by a woman of higher social standing than he is, and, where another man may have turned her down out of embarrassment, Gilbert accepts.

HELEN'S BEDROOM DOOR

> There was, in [Anne] an immense, a terrifying audacity. Charlotte was bold, and Emily was bolder; but this audacity of Anne's was greater than Charlotte's boldness or than Emily's, because it was willed, it was deliberate, open-eyed; [...] Anne took her courage in both hands when she sat down to write *The Tenant of Wildfell Hall*. There are scenes, there are situations, in Anne's amazing novel, which for sheer audacity stand alone in mid-Victorian literature, and which would hold their own in the literature of revolt that followed. [...] Thackeray [...] would have shrunk from recording Mrs. Huntingdon's ultimatum to her husband. The slamming of that bedroom door fairly resounds through the long emptiness of Anne's novel.[41]

That statement comes from May Sinclair's biography, *The Three Brontës*. While she states her opinion that Anne, unlike her sisters, is not a genius, she recognised that Anne's approach to literature was powerful and deliberate. Especially when it came to those issues that she was most passionate about. 'The slamming of that bedroom door...' refers to the part of the novel where Helen shuts her husband out of her bedroom, breaking the law of the time that appropriated a woman to her husband as sexual property:

> Without another word, I left the room, and locked myself up in my own chamber. In about half an hour, he came to the door; and first he tried the handle, then he knocked.
>
> 'Won't you let me in, Helen?' said he.
>
> 'No; you have displeased me,' I replied, 'and I don't want to see your face or hear your voice again till the morning.'
>
> He paused a moment, as if dumbfoundered or uncertain how to answer such a speech, and then turned and walked away.[42]

Huntingdon assumes that Helen's door will be open and tries the handle first. By locking her door, Helen was asserting a right to autonomy over her own body within the marriage. This was illegal, and Anne would have known that at the time she was writing.

Married women in the time of the Brontës had next to no legal rights. They were unable to own property, as they themselves were considered the property of their husbands. Anything that belonged to the wife belonged to her husband. William Blackstone, a prominent legal expert of the eighteenth century, defined this principal of coverture, the idea that a woman was a bond-servant to her husband, in these terms:

> In marriage the husband and wife are one person in law: that is, the very being or legal existence of the woman is

> suspended during the marriage, or at least is incorporated and consolidated into that of the husband under whose wing, protection, and cover, she performs everything […] For this reason, a man cannot grant anything to his wife, or enter into covenant with her: for the grant would suppose her separate existence; and to covenant with her, but be only to covenant with himself.[43]

When she married Arthur Huntingdon, Helen became his property, as did all of her possessions.

Wildfell Hall, especially Helen's Diary, reads as a negative critique of the marriage laws of the time. Even when Helen learns that Arthur no longer cares for her and is, in fact, having an affair with Lady Lowborough, Arthur refuses to grant her a separation.

> 'Well! – what then?' said he, with the calm insolence of mingled shamelessness and desperation.
>
> 'Only this,' returned I: ' Will you let me take our child and what remains of my fortune, and go?'
>
> 'Go where?'
>
> 'Anywhere, where he will be safe from your contaminating influence, and I shall be delivered from your presence – and you from mine.'
>
> 'No – by *Jove* I won't!'
>
> 'Will you let me have the child then, without the money?'
>
> 'No – nor yourself without the child. Do you think I'm going to be made the talk of the country, for your fastidious caprices?'
>
> 'Then I must stay here, to be hated and despised – But henceforth, we are husband and wife in only the name.'
>
> 'Very good.'

> 'I am your child's mother, and *your* housekeeper – nothing more. So you need not trouble yourself any longer, to feign the love you cannot feel; I will exact no more heartless caresses from you – nor offer – nor endure them either – I will not be mocked with the empty husk of conjugal endearments, when you have given the substance to another!'[44]

Helen cannot legally leave her husband unless he initiates the separation, nor can she take her child with her without his permission. Until the first Infant Custody Act of 1839, any woman who lived separately from her husband had to obey her husband's wishes regarding how often, if at all, she could see any children that they had together. Helen becomes gradually more worried about the future of her son as her husband and his friends start trying to 'make a man out of him' for fun, so leaving her child behind was never an option for Helen, as it would have been for many mothers at that time.

Since it wasn't legal for women to separate from their husbands, women were often encouraged to do whatever it took to keep their husbands in good temper.[45] Helen tries to do this earlier in her marriage, but eventually and inevitably fails – Anne takes the very modern view that it shouldn't fall purely on the wife's shoulders to keep a marriage intact. Helen even warns young Esther Hargrave against making the same mistake that she has made: '"[...] stand firm. You might as well sell yourself to slavery at once, as marry a man you dislike. If your mother and brother are unkind to you, you may leave them, but remember you are bound to your husband for life."'[46] Helen notices very early on that her husband is selfish, but she still manages to excuse his actions, until he starts to endanger their son and has an affair. It is at this point that she decides that she must leave.

Helen was breaking societal norms (and the law) when she left Arthur Huntingdon and took her child. She was also committing theft when she sold her paintings – the money she takes with her, the art supplies she purchases, and subsequently the art she makes, all belong to her husband. In selling them and earning her living, not only is she stealing from her husband, but she is doing so in order to fund her unlawful lifestyle. To the modern reader, Helen's escape comes as a relief, a triumph for Helen and her young son. Contemporary readers, however, would have been deeply shocked. I don't think anyone would have agreed with Arthur's treatment of Helen (indeed, many critics condemned the coarse villains created by Anne), but they would have been torn at her decision to leave. By the point Helen leaves, however, she has reached the limit of what she can endure – Arthur's behaviour is what we would now categorise as domestic abuse.

A law that targeted people who psychologically and emotionally abuse their partners, spouses, or family members came into force in the UK in 2015 under the Serious Crime Act. In January 2019, it was announced that Ireland would be introducing a similar law under the Domestic Violence Act. What counts as psychological or emotional abuse? It must be calculated, and it can include coercive and controlling behaviour. That might mean isolating people, controlling what they do and who they spend time with, repeatedly putting them down, and enforcing rules and activities that degrade or dehumanise the victim. The abuse must be continuous for a case to be considered, and it must have had a serious effect on the victim.

If these laws had been in place when Anne was writing *Wildfell Hall*, we could have ended up with a very different novel. Helen is repeatedly made to feel like her husband's bad behaviour is her fault, either for neglecting him too much, or for nagging him too much – she can't win. 'I am so determined to love him –' writes Helen in her journal, 'so intensely anxious to excuse his errors, that I am continually dwelling upon them, and labouring to extenuate the loosest of his principles and the worst of his practices, till I am familiarised with vice and almost a partaker in his sins.'[47]

Almost immediately after the return from a rushed honeymoon, Arthur leaves his new wife alone at home while he spends 'a few days' in London. Those few days turn into weeks, and his letters become less frequent and more terse, until he returns, causing Helen much pain on seeing how ill he has become (it's of his own making – Arthur Huntingdon's hangovers are possibly the most dramatic in literature). Helen learns to be sweet towards him when he comes home from this London trips, nurses him back to health, becomes his angel

'Nameless and Friendless', by Emily Mary Osborn, 1857. This young woman attempting to sell her art mirrors Helen's predicament.

once again, and then he leaves. This cycle continues, until he starts to invite his friends to their home, where a new kind of humiliation starts for Helen. Again, she acts as a glorified babysitter to her husband, catering to his every need and anticipating his wants before he even recognises them himself:

> He likes to have me near him; and, though he is peevish and testy with his servants and his dogs, he is gentle and kind to me. What he would be, if I did not so watchfully anticipate his wants, and so carefully avoid, or immediately desist from doing anything that has a tendency to irritate or disturb him, with however little reason, I cannot tell.[48]

Arthur gradually pushes Helen's patience further as time goes on; when they have a son, he is jealous of the boy for stealing Helen's affections from him. When he invites his friends to stay, he flirts with Lady Lowborough in front of her, and proceeds to make a fool of himself. Even his friends take note of his terrible neglect of his wife and the humiliation he subjects her to, and one of them asks the 'double-dyed scoundrel' to 'turn over a new leaf'. Mr Hargrave relates to Helen her husband's response:

> '"My wife! What wife? I have no wife," replied Huntingdon, looking innocently up from his glass – "or if I have, look you gentlemen, I value her so highly that any one among you, that can fancy her, may have her and welcome – you may, by Jove and my blessing into the bargain!"'[49]

It's a thoroughly degrading appraisal of Helen, made worse by the fact that Hargrave himself is interested in Helen. Through the course of Helen's diary, Hargrave first appears as a possible threat, then a potential ally, and then, after Arthur says that any man can have her, he becomes a threat once again. No matter how often Helen tells him that she is not interested, he refuses to leave her alone, even threatening rape (the emphasis in the following is my own): '"I will be your consoler and defender! And if your conscience upbraid you for it, say I overcame you and *you could not choose but yield!*"'[50] Thankfully, Helen plans an escape both from Arthur and his companions.

In what is possibly Arthur's worst act of abuse towards Helen, he completely invades her privacy and reads her diary. He quickly becomes bored of it, saying that it is too long, and heads to the library. He proceeds to throw her art materials into the fire and orders a servant to discard of her easels.

When Helen does leave, and settles into Wildfell Hall, she carries the fear of being discovered with her – Arthur's abuse has had a 'serious effect on the victim'. She is startled by Gilbert meeting her in the fields, and again when he appears behind her as she paints a cliff scene. She never leaves her child behind at Wildfell Hall with a servant, as Mrs Markham suggests that she should, and she worries about the influence of others on her son. Thankfully for Helen, she has a brother watching out for her, and she doesn't have to live in fear for long.

Anne's characters and their situations still resonate with us today, almost two centuries later. Her eye for observation, and her preoccupation with justice for those who are unable to claim it for themselves gives her work a timeless quality. While it can be argued that *Agnes Grey* and *The Tenant of Wildfell Hall* simply expose what life was like for the middle-class Victorian woman, Anne's characters face many of the same struggles that people do today. The fact that emotional abuse laws are only just starting to come into force are proof of that.

On a positive note, education has come a long way since Anne's time; women are now allowed to attend university and earn degrees, and some important conversations are being had about what it means to be a 'manly' man, and how, to paraphrase Mary Wollstonecraft, justice for women means justice for all. There is surely a long way to go in terms of other minority groups, but in terms of what Anne was fighting for, progress is being made.

SEVEN

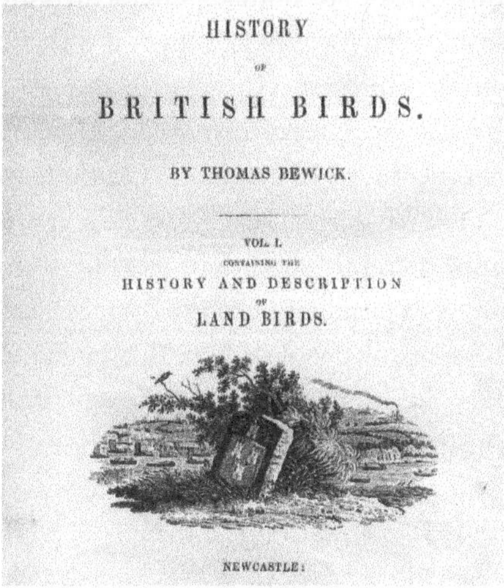
HISTORY

OF

BRITISH BIRDS.

BY THOMAS BEWICK.

VOL. I.

CONTAINING THE

HISTORY AND DESCRIPTION

OF

LAND BIRDS.

NEWCASTLE:

READING LIKE A BRONTË

One of the biggest, and most unfair, misconceptions about the Brontës is that they were completely cut off from the outside world. Both of their parents were incredibly sociable people and made plenty of friends, some of whom became godparents to the Brontë children. Anne's godparents, Elizabeth Firth and Fanny Outhwaite, both kept in touch with the family, offering financial help when they thought it was necessary and sending gifts to the children.

All the girls had experience of formal education, and Charlotte and Emily even spent time in Belgium – Charlotte was there for two years in total. Anne spent five years as a governess to the Robinson family, spending about four weeks a year back home with her family. As a result, none of the Brontës were as short of life experiences as many people believe them to have been.

The idea that the Brontës were complete hermits with wild imaginations has managed to remain a popular idea, however, and often people will ask where the Brontës found their inspiration, how they were able to write about romantic, or passionate, love without ever having experienced it, for example. We know that Charlotte at least felt an intense unrequited love for her teacher in Belgium, Constantin Héger. And Branwell had an alleged affair with his employer's wife, who later rejected him, sending him into a state of despair from which he never recovered.

All the Brontës have been accused at some point of using Branwell as their model for the unsavoury men in their novels – the abusers and alcoholics, such as Heathcliff and Arthur Huntingdon. But that is an extremely unfair appraisal of the imaginative powers of the sisters. They were exposed to men like Heathcliff and Huntingdon much earlier, in the books that they read.

Patrick Brontë enjoyed reading and passed the habit on to his children. He actively encouraged it, supplying his children with textbooks, and trusting them with his own books, such as his classical texts from Cambridge. Books were an expensive commodity, and most of the books owned by the Brontës were second-hand. The Brontës also made use of the Keighley circulating library, too. There was a library at Ponden Hall that they were invited to use, and if they used the Keighley Mechanics Institute Library, they would have had to rely on Patrick and Branwell to borrow books for them (women were not allowed to).

The Brontës had many literary heroes and influences, not limited to the ones looked at here. Many veteran writers of fiction advise aspiring young writers to read as much as they can, as often as they can, and the Brontës were no exception to this rule.

TEXTBOOKS

The Brontës owned some of the standard educational texts of the day, including *A History of England* by Oliver Goldsmith, *Ancient History* by Charles Rollin, *A New Geographical and Historical Grammar* by Thomas Salmon, and *A Grammar of General Geography* by J. Goldsmith.[1] All of the books are now very hard to find. Copies of the last two are still held at the Brontë Parsonage Museum (on their website, there is an option to download a list of books that were owned by the Brontë family and which contained annotations by them).

A Grammar of General Geography was notably prized by the Brontë children – the maps and descriptions of faraway foreign lands inspired some of their plays, the settings and names of their imaginary kingdoms, and their own map-making attempts. Anne even added a list of her Gondal and Gaaldine place names to the book:

> Alexandria, A kingdom in Gaaldine.
> Almedore, a kingdom in Gaaldine.

> Elseraden, a kingdom in Gaaldine.
> Gaaldine, a large Island newly discovered in the South Pacific,
> Gondal, a large Island in the North Pacific.
> Regina, the capital of Gondal.
> Ula, a kingdom in Gaaldine, governed by 4 Sovereigns.
> Zelona, a kingdom in Gaaldine.
> Zedora, a large Provence in Gaaldine Governed by a Viceroy.[2]

The Brontës also made use of Patrick's collection of classical works, including Homer's *Iliad*. William Makepeace Thackeray said of *Jane Eyre*, 'Who the author can be I can't guess; if a woman she knows her language better than most ladies do, or has had a classical education.'[3] Charlotte was familiar with translations from the classics, even if she couldn't read them in Greek or Latin, while Emily and Anne were adept enough at Latin to be able to translate passages and also teach it. Emily translated and made notes on Virgil's *Aeneid*, and Anne was able to teach Edmund Robinson some Latin before Branwell became his tutor.

The household also owned a copy of Hannah More's *Moral Sketches of Prevailing Opinions and Manners*, which was annotated by Patrick. In a chapter titled 'On the Exertions of Pious Ladies', she warns against performing Christian duties purely for the sake of being seen to be doing so. The book comes across as an exercise in extreme self-awareness, almost to the point of self-consciousness. It's highly interesting as a book of its time, but thankfully, the Brontës had more entertaining things to read too.

One of their well-loved books was Thomas Bewick's *A History of British Birds*, which all the Brontës loved. The illustrations, in particular, were a much-admired feature, and the children would copy them. Bewick's book appears most famously in *Jane Eyre* when Jane describes the impressions that Bewick made on her young mind, firing her imagination with its suggestions of exotic and romantic landscapes: 'Each picture told a story; mysterious often to my undeveloped understanding and imperfect feelings, yet ever profoundly interesting [...] With Bewick on my knee, I was then happy: happy at least in my way. I feared nothing but interruption, and that came too soon.'[4]

THE BIBLE

The parsonage library contained multiple copies and editions of the Bible, plus books of common prayer, hymn books, and religious pamphlets containing sermons. All the Brontës read and studied the Bible, as did most educated children at the time. Anne undertook an eighteen-month study of her Bible (which had been given to her by her godmother, Elizabeth Firth), making annotations and notes around those passages that most helped her through her own religious doubts.

The Bible is the most quoted text in *Wildfell Hall*, and also, surprisingly, in *Jane Eyre*. Mr Brocklehurst asks Jane if she reads the Bible. Jane says yes: "I like Revelations, and the book of Daniel, and Genesis and Samuel, and a little bit of Exodus, and some parts of Kings and Chronicles, and Job and Jonah."[5] Mr Brocklehurst then asks if she enjoys the psalms, to which she replies no. He then calls her a wicked girl. The parts of the Bible that Jane professes to enjoy are from the Old Testament, the more narrative-driven, heroic and prophetic parts. Later, Helen Burns advises her that she should read the New Testament and learn from Christ about forgiving and loving your enemies. St John Rivers also mainly references the New Testament, mostly the writings of Paul, who was also a missionary.

Bibles and prayer books were not the only religious writings that the Brontës had access to – their mother or aunt brought with them from Penzance some copies of *The Wesleyan Methodist Magazine*. These make an appearance in Charlotte's *Shirley*: Caroline Helstone finds in the Rectory library 'some mad Methodist Magazines, full of miracles and apparitions, of preternatural warnings, ominous dreams, and frenzied fanaticism'.[6] They must have had an influence on the impressionable and imaginative young Brontës.

William Cowper was a religious poet and writer of hymns, and Anne and Branwell, in particular, were big fans of his – Anne even dedicated a poem to him (see Chapter Five). She felt that his poems were representative of her own religious doubts and fear of losing faith. Anne, too, wrote some hymns, labelling them in her manuscripts as such. Her hymns have since made it into Methodist, Baptist and Anglican collections of hymns.

Doré's dramatic image of Lot, from the Book of Genesis.

THE PILGRIM'S PROGRESS

Anne Brontë's best-known hymn was likely inspired by John Bunyan's *The Pilgrim's Progress*:

> Believe not those who say
> The upward path is smooth,
> Lest thou shouldst stumble in the way
> And faint before the truth. [...]
>
> Arm, arm thee for the fight!
> Cast useless loads away:
> Watch through the darkest hours of night;
> Toil through the hottest day.
>
> Crush pride into the dust,
> Or thou must needs be slack;
> And trample down rebellious lust,
> Or it will hold thee back.[7]

Bunyan's allegorical tale, published in 1678, has never been out of print. It is considered to be one of the most important works of religious English literature, and was cherished by the young Brontës. It was a favourite of the March sisters in Louisa May Alcott's *Little Women* too; the book opens with them reading *The Pilgrim's Progress* and trying to follow the good example set by the protagonist.

Christian is on a pilgrimage from the 'City of Destruction' (this world) to the 'Celestial City' (heaven) on Mount Zion. Christian must complete his journey while weighed down by the knowledge of his sin. Along the way, he encounters obstacles, and also people who are willing to help him. It is easy to see why such a story would appeal to Anne; many of her religious poems follow a similar theme. The narrator laments that the path before them is difficult, but then finds hope in the idea that their faith will help them find the way and, ultimately, will lead them to heaven. The first three verses of 'Confidence', written by Anne in 1845, follow this pattern of beginning a journey to God while weighed down by sin:

Oppressed with sin and woe,
A burdened heart I bear,
Opposed by many a mighty foe:
But I will not despair.

With this polluted heart
I dare to come to Thee,
Holy and mighty as Thou art;
For Thou wilt pardon me.

I feel that I am weak,
And prone to every sin:
But Thou who giv'st to those who seek,
Wilt give me strength within.[8]

The Pilgrim's Progress is, essentially, a dream sequence: the reader follows Christian as he casts aside his burden of sin, converses with angels, avoids lions and makes it through the Slough of Despond. Anyone who has read or seen Michael Ende's *The Neverending Story* will be able to guess at the purpose of the Slough of Despond – much like the Swamps of Sadness in Ende's story, the Slough of Despond is a boggy swamp where Christian must battle his doubts, shame, guilt and sins that try to sink him. It's almost surreal, and you can see why the Brontës would have enjoyed it.

'Christian reading in his book' – an illustration by William Blake for The Pilgrim's Progress.

PARADISE LOST

The Brontës' own copy of John Milton's *Paradise Lost: a poem in twelve books* has annotations and markings by Charlotte, but it was read by all of them. It tells the story of the biblical Fall of Man: the temptation by Satan of Adam and Eve – to entice them to eat the forbidden fruit – and their expulsion from Eden. The poem looks daunting, but Philip Pullman has some excellent advice for reading it: try not to look too deeply the first time around, read the poem aloud (or have it read to you!), and enjoy the story. He illustrates this point with the story of a man who listens 'transfixed' to *Paradise Lost* being read aloud: 'Suddenly he bangs the arm of his chair, and exclaims "By God! I know not what the outcome may be, but this Lucifer is a damned fine fellow, and I hope he may win!"'[9]

And that's the point of *Paradise Lost* – you find yourself rooting for Lucifer, much in the same way as fans of Neil Gaiman and Terry Pratchett's *Good Omens* root for an angel and a demon who aren't really on anybody's side. What if the Fall of Man was part of God's master plan? And was Lucifer right to rebel against a regime that he didn't agree with and couldn't follow? Readers of *Paradise Lost* side with Lucifer because he is the first character the reader comes into contact with; he has just been expelled from heaven, flung into the sulphurous fumes and fiery agonies of hell. He is easy to sympathise with, and already the reader's expectations have been toyed with. In this story, the devil is the hero.

There are at least two references to *Paradise Lost* in *Jane Eyre*: one when Rochester is inspecting Jane's paintings, which are inspired by the book; and the second is when he implies to Jane that he is a great sinner who has been permanently expelled from heaven. When discussing Jane's paintings, both Jane and Rochester appear to be equally knowledgeable about *Paradise Lost*, and Jane's third painting depicts Death as he is described in the poem. Jane's painting showed:

> Two thin hands, joined under the forehead, and supporting it, drew up before the lower features a sable veil; a brow quite bloodless, white as bone, and an eye hollow and fixed, blank of meaning but for the glassiness of despair, alone were visible. Above the temples, amidst wreathed turban folds of black drapery, vague in its character and consistency as cloud, gleamed a ring of white flame, gemmed with sparkles of a more lurid tinge. This pale crescent was 'the likeness of a kingly crown;' what it diademed was 'the shape which shape had none.'[10]

Paradise Lost describes Death as:

The other shape,
If shape it might be called that shape had none
Distinguishable in member, joint, or limb,
Or substance might be called that shadow seemed,
For each seemed either; black it stood as Night,
Fierce as ten Furies, terrible as Hell,
And shook a dreadful Dart; what seem'd his head
The likeness of a Kingly Crown had on[11]

THE ROMANTIC POETS

The Brontës were very familiar with the works of the Romantics: Wordsworth, Coleridge, Shelley, Southey and Byron were the best loved among them. Romantic poetry tended towards the exploration of the interior world of feeling. The poets that most moved the Brontës were those who found parallels to their emotional lives in the natural world, Wordsworth's famous example being 'I Wandered Lonely as a Cloud'. Romantic poetry was full of powerful and spontaneous feelings, which Charlotte, Branwell and Emily enjoyed.

Wuthering Heights took inspiration from the Romantics in the portrayal of nature as a living, vitalising thing; it isn't just portrayed as tranquil and a source of joy, but the darker, stormier moods of nature are presented, too. Cathy's most famous line compares her relationships with Heathcliff and Edgar Linton to two wildly different aspects of nature:

> My love for Linton is like the foliage in the woods: time will change it, I'm well aware, as winter changes the trees. My love for Heathcliff resembles the eternal rocks beneath: a source of little visible delight, but necessary.[12]

Heathcliff himself is a Byronic hero. What is a Byronic hero? They are not always necessarily likeable characters (like in the case of Heathcliff). They are generally melancholic, their motives are not always made clear to others, and they lack family ties thanks to their mysterious origins. They are isolated but seek to change this through almost obsessive love. These are characteristics that were common to many of the heroes in Charlotte and Branwell's Glass Town and Angria tales.

Byron was adored by the Brontës: Charlotte copied his portrait numerous times, they all read his poem *Don Juan*, and Thomas Moore's *The Life of Lord Byron* was almost as interesting to them as his poems. Anyone who has wondered where characters like Heathcliff and Rochester could have come from needs look no further than the works and life of Lord Byron. His heroes were rakes and rogues, as was he; his life was even more colourful than the fictions he invented. He toured Europe extensively, was involved in numerous scandals, and was famously described by Lady Caroline Lamb, a former lover, as 'mad, bad, and dangerous to know'. It's no wonder the Brontës were fascinated by him. He was one of the first modern celebrities, and newspapers would keep up with his exploits even when he wasn't in the country.

Winifred Gérin even suggests that Emily was inspired by Byron's own journals, given that her Diary Papers were 'begun as ill-written, ill-spelt, blotted, crumpled exercises to a pattern first suggested by Byron'.[13] As Gérin points out, extracts from Byron's personal journal do appear in Moore's *The Life of Lord Byron*, and so Emily could have read them and copied their style.

Charlotte and Branwell each wrote to a Romantic poet to ask for advice as aspiring writers. Charlotte wrote to Robert Southey, and Branwell wrote to William Wordsworth, and both sent examples of their poetry. Branwell never received a reply

– Wordsworth was disgusted by his obvious flattery and the verse that was too obviously influenced by Wordsworth himself. Charlotte did receive a (now infamous) reply.

Southey praised Charlotte's talents as a writer but warned her against becoming absorbed in an imaginary world that was in danger of taking over the real one. This would have been good advice on its own, but Southey went on to say, 'Literature cannot be the business of a woman's life: and it ought not to be. The more she is engaged in her proper duties, the less leisure she will have for it, even as an accomplishment & a recreation.'[14] Charlotte wrote back to thank him for the advice, but fortunately for us, she failed to follow it.

SIR WALTER SCOTT

Ellen Nussey once asked Charlotte in a letter for some book recommendations and her response included praise of Sir Walter Scott's 'sweet, wild, romantic poetry' and the assertion that 'all novels after his are worthless'.[15]

Sir Walter Scott was a Scottish poet and novelist whose most famous works include the novels *Ivanhoe* and *Rob Roy* and the poem 'The Lady of the Lake'. Patrick Brontë owned a copy of 'The Lay of the Last Minstrel', and Charlotte was presented with a copy of 'The Vision of Don Roderick' by Miss Wooler when she was at Roe Head. Charlotte became a huge fan of Scott – it was in his novels and poems that she first became obsessed with love as a romantic concept.

Emily and Anne were inspired by Scott's works in their creation of Gondal; the northern landscape of Gondal is much closer to the landscape of Haworth than it is to that of Angria, but the northern mountains and the wooded hills present in Gondal are also reminiscent of the Scottish Borders as described in Scott's works. Not only did they take inspiration from his scenery, but they borrowed his characters and storylines too. Even the characters have Scottish names: Ronald and Flora Stewart, Una Campbell, Helen Douglas, for example.[16]

Scott even appears in *Wildfell Hall*. Gilbert Markham, after talking about books with Helen, discovers that she has long wanted to read Scott's 'Marmion'. Gilbert procures an attractive copy of it and presents it to Helen as a gift, after carrying it around with him all day.[17] Even if you aren't familiar with the title, you will be familiar with these two lines from the poem: 'Oh! what a tangled web we weave / When first we practise to deceive!'

Bridge from The Lady of the Lake, by Sir Walter Scott (illustrations: Birket Foster and John Wood). The landscape around Scott's home in the Scottish Borders influenced the Brontës' ideas of landscape.

Lord Byron was one of the Brontës' favourite poets.

BLACKWOOD'S MAGAZINE

The impact of *Blackwood's Magazine* on the Brontës cannot be overstated. It suited their tastes perfectly; its version of satire blended politics and current affairs with literature in a way that was irresistible to them. It's hard to imagine a modern-day equivalent. Perhaps part *Private Eye*, part *New Yorker*, part *Literary Review*, but even then, that's not getting close.

The heroes of the magazine became their heroes – the Duke of Wellington and Lord Byron being two such examples. The long reviews of new books that appeared in *Blackwood's* also gave them access to otherwise inaccessible knowledge, and it showed them how they could combine their interests, inspiring what was to become 'The Young Men's Magazine', which was a parody of *Blackwood's* written by Charlotte and Branwell in miniature books. Their magazine contained contents pages, prose fiction, 'conversations', poetry and even advertisements. 'The Young Men's Magazine' of October 1830 announced on its title page: 'SOLD BY SERGEANT TREE AND ALL OTHER Booksellers in the Glass Town, Paris, Ross's Glass Town, Parry's G Town & the Duke of Wellington's Glass Town'.[18]

AFTERWORD

In July 2019 the final stone in the Brontë Stones Project, the Anne stone, was laid behind Haworth Parsonage, in the Parson's Field. The project, devised and put together by the writer Michael Stewart for the bicentenary celebrations, saw Carol Ann Duffy, Jeanette Winterson, Kate Bush and Jackie Kay write new poems about the Brontës. The poems were carved into stones that have been placed at key points along a nine-mile walk between Haworth Parsonage and the Brontë birthplace in Thornton.

When Jackie Kay, the Scottish Makar (Poet Laureate), was asked which Brontë she would most like to write a poem for, her first reaction was Anne. She has said in interviews that 'Anne was the one who is often overlooked and is the outsider in her own family. She is a feminist and is much more radical than her sisters, despite being seen as a pale reflection of them.'[1] Jackie wanted to write a poem that illustrated how Anne's sisters – and, indeed, the rest of the world – have misread and misunderstood Anne for years:

> These **dark** sober clothes
> are my disguise. No, I was not preparing
> for an early death, yours or mine.
> You got me all **wrong**, all the time.
> But sisters, I will have the last word,
> write the last line. I am **still** at sea –
> but if I can do some good in this world

I will right the **wrong**. I am **still** young,
and the moor's winds lift my light-**dark** hair.
I am **still here** when the sun goes up,
and **here** when the moon drops down.
I do not now stand alone.

Jackie Kay, 2018

The stone itself is in the top right-hand corner of Parson's Field. To read the poem, you have to stand behind the stone, with your back against the wall of the field, so that you can see the corner of the parsonage poking out from between the trees. It's a touching tribute to Anne, the only Brontë not to be buried with her family in the Haworth church. The only way to read the poem is to face the home she spent so much time away from, the home she came back to in order to write her novels.

Jackie Kay has said that she wanted to write a poem within a poem. If you stand in front of the stone, you can see that some words have been carved differently than others. Words like 'still', 'wrong' and 'still here' are bold, reminding us to be mindful of Anne as a real person, more complex than any interpretation of her could fully represent. Charlotte's 'Biographical Notice of Ellis and Acton Bell' appears in almost every edition of *Wuthering Heights*, perpetuating ideas about Anne's personality, talents and motivation for writing that are 'still wrong'. Her works are 'still here', waiting to be found, waiting to be read while popular culture continues to pass over her as the boring Brontë.

Even the colour of her hair is a matter of dispute – some sources describe her hair as fair, others as a darker brown – and Jackie refers to Anne's 'light-dark hair' in her poem. It's just another misunderstanding in a life that has been almost completely misunderstood, even by those closest to her. In encouraging us to dig deeper and find her hidden poem, Jackie urges us to do the same with Anne, to challenge our perceptions, sympathise with her, and humanise her a little more.

The more I learn about Anne, the more I understand that if you are incapable of speaking for yourself, then others will do it for you. And it will probably be a very long time before they get it right.

NOTES & REFERENCES

INTRODUCTION

1. Muriel Spark, *The Essence of The Brontës*, Carcanet, Manchester, 2014, p.8
2. Unsigned review in *Douglas Jerrold's Weekly Newspaper*, 15 January 1848: see Miriam Allott, *The Brontës: The Critical Heritage*, Routledge, London, 2001, p.227
3. Unsigned review in *The Spectator*: see Juliet Barker, *The Brontës*, Abacus, London, 2010, p.665
4. Lucasta Miller, *The Brontë Myth*, Anchor Books, New York, 2005, p.xiii

CHAPTER ONE: THE LIFE AND WORKS OF ANNE

1. Juliet Barker, *The Brontës*, Abacus, London, 2010, pp.99–101
2. Marianne Thormählen, 'Anne Brontë and her Bible', *Brontë Studies*, 37:4, pp.339–344, 2012
3. Juliet Barker, *The Brontës*, Abacus, London, 2010, p.148
4. *Ibid*, p.149
5. Edward Chitham, *A Life of Anne Brontë*, Blackwell Publishers, Oxford, 1991, p.17
6. *Ibid*, p.16
7. Sarah Garrs, quoted by Marion Harland in 'Charlotte Brontë at Home': see Juliet Barker, *The Brontës: A Life in Letters*, Little, Brown, London, 2016, p.3
8. Juliet Barker, *The Brontës*, Abacus, London, 2010, p.119
9. Elizabeth Gaskell, *The Life of Charlotte Brontë*, Oxford University Press, Oxford, 1996, p.41
10. *Ibid*, p.43
11. *Ibid*, p.49
12. *Ibid*, p.47
13. Juliet Barker, *The Brontës*, Abacus, London, 2010, p.127
14. Elizabeth Gaskell, *The Life of Charlotte Brontë*, Oxford University Press, Oxford, 1996, pp.47–48
15. Juliet Barker, *The Brontës: A Life in Letters*, Little, Brown, London, 2016, pp.10–11
16. From Charlotte Brontë's 'The History of the Year', written on 12 March 1829: see Juliet Barker, *The Brontës: A Life in Letters*, Little, Brown, London, 2016, p.12
17. Christine Alexander, *The Brontës: Tales of Glass Town, Angria and Gondal*, Oxford University Press, Oxford, 2010, pp.494–495
18. Miss Ellen Nussey, 'Reminiscences of Charlotte Brontë', *Brontë Society Transactions*, 2:10, pp.58–83, 1899
19. Winifred Gérin, *Anne Brontë: A Biography*, Allen Lane, London, 1976, p.80

20. Juliet Barker, *The Brontës*, Abacus, London, 2010, p.295
21. Winifred Gérin, *Anne Brontë: A Biography*, Allen Lane, London, 1976, p.86
22. Edward Chitham, *The Poems of Anne Brontë: A New Text and Commentary*, Macmillan Press, London, 1979, p.61
23. Juliet Barker, *The Brontës*, Abacus, London, 2010, p.322
24. Elizabeth Gaskell, *The Life of Charlotte Brontë*, Oxford University Press, Oxford, 1996, p.131
25. Juliet Barker, *The Brontës*, Abacus, London, 2010, p.327
26. Ibid, p.359
27. Edward Chitham, *A Life of Anne Brontë*, Blackwell Publishers, Oxford, 1991, p.58
28. Charlotte Brontë to Ellen Nussey, 15 April 1839: see Juliet Barker, *The Brontës: A Life in Letters*, Little, Brown, London, 2016, pp.63–64
29. Edward Chitham, *A Life of Anne Brontë*, Blackwell Publishers, Oxford, 1991, p.60
30. Juliet Barker, *The Brontës*, Abacus, London, 2010, p.372
31. Edward Chitham, *A Life of Anne Brontë*, Blackwell Publishers, Oxford, 1991, pp.62–63
32. Juliet Barker, *The Brontës*, Abacus, London, 2010, p.380
33. *Ibid*, p.381
34. *Ibid*, p.473
35. Edward Chitham, *A Life of Anne Brontë*, Blackwell Publishers, Oxford, 1991, pp.78–83
36. Juliet Barker, *The Brontës*, Abacus, London, 2010, p.171
37. Anne Brontë's Diary Paper, 30 July 1841: see Christine Alexander, *The Brontës: Tales of Glass Town, Angria and Gondal*, Oxford University Press, Oxford, 2010, pp.489–490
38. Anne Brontë's Diary Paper, 31 July 1845, see Christine Alexander, *The Brontës: Tales of Glass Town*, Angria and Gondal, Oxford University Press, Oxford, 2010, pp.492–493
39. *Ibid*, pp.490–491
40. *Ibid*, p.492
41. Charlotte Brontë to Ellen Nussey, 28 July 1848: see Juliet Barker, *The Brontës: A Life in Letters*, Little, Brown, London, 2016, p.201
42. Charlotte Brontë to William Smith Williams, 7 December 1848: see Juliet Barker, *The Brontës: A Life in Letters*, Little, Brown, London, 2016, p.215
43. Charlotte Brontë to Ellen Nussey, 28 July 1848: see Juliet Barker, *The Brontës: A Life in Letters*, Little, Brown, London, 2016, p.201
44. Charlotte Brontë's 'Biographical Notice of Ellis and Acton Bell', in Emily Brontë, *Wuthering Heights*, Penguin Classics, London, 1985, p.30
45. Anne Brontë's Diary Paper, 31 July 1845: see Christine Alexander, *The Brontës: Tales of Glass Town, Angria and Gondal*, Oxford University Press, Oxford, 2010, p.492
46. Daphne du Maurier, *The Infernal World of Branwell Brontë*, Victor Gollancz, London, 1960, p.15
47. Elizabeth Gaskell, *The Life of Charlotte Brontë*, Oxford University Press,

Oxford, 1996, p.300

48. Anne Brontë to Ellen Nussey, 5 April 1849: see Juliet Barker, *The Brontës: A Life in Letters*, Little, Brown, London, 2016, pp.228–229
49. Ellen Nussey's 'Reminiscences of Charlotte Brontë': see Juliet Barker, *The Brontës: A Life in Letters*, Little, Brown, London, 2016, p.232
50. *Ibid*, pp.233–235
51. *Ibid*, p.235

CHAPTER TWO: ACTON BELL

1. Edward Chitham, *A Life of Anne Brontë*, Blackwell, 1991, p.5
2. Anne Brontë, *Agnes Grey*, Penguin Classics, London, 1988, p.142
3. Edward Chitham, *The Poems of Anne Brontë: A New Text and Commentary*, Macmillan Press, London, 1979, pp.49–51
4. Winifred Gérin, *Anne Brontë: A Biography*, Allen Lane, 1976, p.91
5. Edward Chitham, *The Poems of Anne Brontë: A New Text And Commentary*, Macmillan, London, 1979, pp.60–61
6. Christine Alexander, *The Brontës: Tales of Glass Town, Angria and Gondal*, Oxford University Press, Oxford, 2010, p.xxxv
7. Anne Brontë, *Agnes Grey*, Penguin Classics, London, 1988, p.142
8. Anne Brontë, *The Tenant of Wildfell Hall*, Penguin Classics, London, 1996, p.4
9. Edward Chitham, *The Poems of Anne Brontë: A New Text and Commentary*, Macmillan Press, London, 1979, pp.34–39
10. *Ibid*, p.36
11. *Ibid*, pp.115–119
12. *Ibid*, pp.144–150
13. *Ibid*, pp.152–160
14. Edward Chitham, *The Poems of Anne Brontë: A New Text and Commentary*, Macmillan Press, London, 1979, p.159
15. Samantha Ellis, *Take Courage: Anne Brontë and the Art of Life*, Chatto and Windus, London, 2017, pp.112–113
16. Edward Chitham, *The Poems of Anne Brontë: A New Text and Commentary*, Macmillan Press, London, 1979, pp.87–88
17. *Ibid*, p.72
18. Samantha Ellis, *Take Courage: Anne Brontë and the Art of Life, Chatto and Windus*, London, 2017, p.178
19. Juliet Barker, *The Brontës*, Abacus, London, 2010, p.429
20. *Ibid*, p.684
21. Elizabeth Gaskell, *The Life of Charlotte Brontë*, Oxford University Press, Oxford, 1996, p.233
22. Juliet Barker, *The Brontës*, Abacus, London, 2010, p.620
23. *Ibid*, p.636
24. *Ibid*
25. Unsigned review in *The Spectator*, 18 December 1847: see Juliet Barker, *The*

Brontës, Abacus, London, 2010, p.637

26. Unsigned review, *Britannia*, 15 January 1848, and unsigned review, *Atlas*, 22 January 1848: see Juliet Barker, *The Brontës*, Abacus, London, 2010, p.638
27. Unsigned review, *Douglas Jerrold's Weekly Newspaper*, 15 January 1848: see Miriam Allott, *The Brontës: The Critical Heritage*, Routledge, London, 2001, p.227
28. Lucy Hughes-Hallett (ed), *Agnes Grey and The Tenant of Wildfell Hall*, Everyman's Library, London, 2012, p.x
29. Anne Brontë, *Agnes Grey*, Penguin Classics, London, 1988, pp.96–97
30. Olivia Laing, *The Lonely City*, Canongate Books, Edinburgh, 2016, p.5
31. Anne Brontë, *Agnes Grey*, Penguin Classics, London, 1988, p.140
32. Lucy Hughes-Hallett (ed), *Agnes Grey and The Tenant of Wildfell Hall*, Everyman's Library, London, 2012, p.x
33. Stevie Davies, '"Three distinct and unconnected tales": The Professor, Agnes Grey and Wuthering Heights', in Heather Glen (ed), *The Cambridge Companion to The Brontës*, Cambridge University Press, Cambridge, 2002, p.84
34. Anne Brontë, *Agnes Grey*, Penguin Classics, London, 1988, p.10
35. *Ibid*, p.xlvii
36. Daphne du Maurier, *The Infernal World of Branwell Brontë*, Victor Gollancz, London, 1960, p.148
37. *Ibid*, p.149
38. From George Moore's *Conversation in Ebury Street*: see Ada Harrison and Derek Stanford, *Anne Brontë – Her Life and Work*, Archon Books, Hamdon, 1970, pp.227–229
39. Stevie Davies, '"Three distinct and unconnected tales": The Professor, Agnes Grey and Wuthering Heights', in Heather Glen (ed), *The Cambridge Companion to The Brontës*, Cambridge University Press, Cambridge, 2002, pp.84–85
40. Elizabeth Gaskell, *The Life of Charlotte Brontë*, Oxford University Press, Oxford, 1996, p.281
41. Unsigned review in *The Spectator*: see Juliet Barker, *The Brontës*, Abacus, London, 2010, p.665
42. Winifred Gérin, *Branwell Brontë: A Biography*, Thomas Nelson, Edinburgh, 1961, p.317
43. Philip Pullman, 'God and Dust: Notes for a study day with the Bishop of Oxford', *Daemon Voices: Essays on Storytelling*, David Fickling Books, Oxford, 2017, p.432

CHAPTER THREE: ANNE EDITED

1. Charlotte Brontë's 'Biographical Notice of Ellis and Acton Bell', in Emily Brontë, *Wuthering Heights*, Penguin Classics, London, 1985, p.36
2. Anne Brontë, *The Tenant of Wildfell Hall*, Penguin Classics, London, 1996,

pp.3–5
3. Charlotte Brontë to William Smith Williams, 5 September 1850: see Juliet Barker, *The Brontës: A Life In Letters*, Little, Brown, London, 2016, p.295
4. Charlotte Brontë's 'Biographical Notice of Ellis and Acton Bell', in Emily Brontë, *Wuthering Heights*, Penguin Classics, London, 1985, p.34
5. G. D. Hargreaves, 'Incomplete Texts Of "The Tenant Of Wildfell Hall"', *Brontë Society Transactions*, 16:2, pp.113–117, 1972
6. Stevie Davies, 'A note on the text', in Anne Brontë, *The Tenant of Wildfell Hall*, Penguin Classics, London, 1996, p.492
7. Samantha Ellis, *Take Courage: Anne Brontë and the Art of Life*, Chatto & Windus, London, 2017, p.143
8. G. D. Hargreaves, 'Incomplete Texts Of "The Tenant Of Wildfell Hall"', *Brontë Society Transactions*, 16:2, pp.113–117, 1972
9. Anne Brontë, *The Tenant of Wildfell Hall*, Penguin Classics, London, 1996, p.10
10. G. D. Hargreaves, 'Further Omissions In "The Tenant Of Wildfell Hall"', *Brontë Society Transactions*, 17:2, pp.115–121, 1977
11. Anne Brontë, *The Tenant of Wildfell Hall*, Penguin Classics, London, 1996, p.399
12. *Ibid*, p.307
13. *Ibid*, p.239
14. *Ibid*, p.240
15. Samantha Ellis, *Take Courage: Anne Brontë and the Art of Life*, Chatto & Windus, London, 2017, p.147
16. *Ibid*, p.1
17. G. D. Hargreaves, 'Further Omissions In "The Tenant Of Wildfell Hall"', *Brontë Society Transactions*, 17:2, pp.115–121, 1977
18. Charlotte Brontë to William Smith Williams, 5 September 1850 and 13 September 1850: see Juliet Barker, *The Brontës: A Life In Letters*, Little, Brown, London, 2016, pp.295–296
19. Juliet Barker, *The Brontës*, Abacus, London, 2010, p.773
20. *Ibid*, p.774
21. Claire O'Callaghan, *Emily Brontë: Reappraised*, Saraband, Salford, 2018, p.82
22. Edward Chitham, *The Poems of Anne Brontë: A New Text and Commentary*, Macmillan Press, London, 1979, p.16
23. *Ibid*, p.110
24. Juliet Barker, *The Brontës: Selected Poems*, Everyman, London, 1993, p.45
25. Edward Chitham, *The Poems of Anne Brontë: A New Text and Commentary*, Macmillan Press, London, 1979, p.81
26. Juliet Barker, *The Brontës: Selected Poems*, Everyman, London, 1993, pp.99–101
27. Juliet Barker, *The Brontës*, Abacus, London, 2010, p.686
28. Elizabeth Gaskell, *The Life of Charlotte Brontë*, Oxford University Press, Oxford, 1996, p.303
29. Juliet Barker, *The Brontës*, Abacus, London, 2010, p.775
30. Charlotte Brontë's 'Biographical Notice of Ellis and Acton Bell', in Emily

Brontë, *Wuthering Heights*, Penguin Classics, London, 1985, p.36
31. Lucasta Miller, *The Brontë Myth*, Anchor Books, New York, 2005, p.149
32. Samantha Ellis, *Take Courage: Anne Brontë and the Art of Life*, Chatto & Windus, London, 2017, p.139
33. Charlotte Brontë's 'Biographical Notice of Ellis and Acton Bell', in Emily Brontë, *Wuthering Heights*, Penguin Classics, London, 1985, p.36
34. *Ibid*
35. Charlotte Brontë to William Smith Williams, 4 June 1849 and 13 June 1849: see Juliet Barker, *The Brontës: A Life In Letters*, Little, Brown, London, 2016, pp.236–237
36. Miss Ellen Nussey, 'Reminiscences of Charlotte Brontë', *Brontë Society Transactions*, 2:10, pp.58–83, 1899
37. Charlotte Brontë to Ellen Nussey, 13 December 1846: see Juliet Barker, *The Brontës: A Life In Letters*, Little, Brown, London, 2016, p.157
38. Charlotte Brontë to Elizabeth Gaskell, 26 September 1850: see Juliet Barker, *The Brontës: A Life In Letters*, Little, Brown, London, 2016, p.299
39. Charlotte Brontë to James Taylor, 22 May 1850: see Juliet Barker, *The Brontës: A Life In Letters*, Little, Brown, London, 2016, p.280
40. Lucasta Miller, *The Brontë Myth*, Anchor Books, New York, 2005, p.xiii
41. Muriel Spark, *The Essence of The Brontës*, Carcanet, Manchester, 2014, p.8
42. Laura L. Hinkley, *The Brontës: Charlotte and Emily*, Hammond, Hammond & Co., London, 1947, p.80
43. Anne Brontë, *Agnes Grey*, Penguin Classics, London, 1988, p.117
44. Elizabeth Gaskell, *The Life of Charlotte Brontë*, Oxford University Press, Oxford, 1996, p.281
45. Winifred Gérin, *Anne Brontë: A Biography*, Allen Lane, London, 1976, p.254
46. Edward Chitham, *The Poems of Anne Brontë: A New Text and Commentary*, Macmillan Press, London, 1979, p.39

CHAPTER FOUR: ANNE IN NATURE

1. Elizabeth Gaskell, *The Life of Charlotte Brontë*, Oxford University Press, Oxford, 1996, p.11
2. Winifred Gérin, *Anne Brontë: A Biography*, Allen Lane, London, 1976, p.60
3. Anne Brontë, *Agnes Grey*, Penguin Classics, London, 1988, p.104
4. *Ibid*
5. *Ibid*, p.105
6. Anne Brontë, *The Tenant of Wildfell Hall*, Penguin Classics, London, 1996, pp.223–224
7. Edward Chitham, *The Poems of Anne Brontë: A New Text and Commentary*, Macmillan Press, London, 1979, p.100
8. *Ibid*, p.74
9. Anne Brontë, *Agnes Grey*, Penguin Classics, London, 1988, p.106

10. Barbara T. Gates, 'Natural History', in Marianne Thormählen (ed), *The Brontës In Context*, Cambridge University Press, 2014, pp.258–259
11. Anne Brontë, *Agnes Grey*, Penguin Classics, London, 1988, p.109
12. *Ibid*, p.151
13. Anne Brontë, *The Tenant of Wildfell Hall*, Penguin Classics, London, 1996, p.482
14. Barbara T. Gates, 'Natural History', in Marianne Thormählen (ed), *The Brontës In Context*, Cambridge University Press, 2014, p.259
15. Anne Brontë, *The Tenant of Wildfell Hall*, Penguin Classics, London, 1996, p.23
16. *Ibid*, p.503
17. *Ibid*, p.91
18. Edward Chitham, *A Life of Anne Brontë*, Blackwell Publishers, Oxford, 1991, p.79
19. Emily and Anne's Diary Paper, 24 November 1834: see Juliet Barker, *The Brontës: A Life In Letters*, Little, Brown, London, 2016, p.29
20. Miss Ellen Nussey, 'Reminiscences of Charlotte Brontë', *Brontë Society Transactions*, 2:10, pp.58–83, 1899
21. Anne's Diary Paper, 30 July 1841: see Christine Alexander, *The Brontës: Tales of Glass Town, Angria and Gondal*, Oxford University Press, Oxford, 2010, p.489
22. Miss Ellen Nussey, 'Reminiscences of Charlotte Brontë', *Brontë Society Transactions*, 2:10, pp.58–83, 1899
23. Anne Brontë to Ellen Nussey, 26 January 1848: see Juliet Barker, *The Brontës: A Life In Letters*, Little, Brown, London, 2016, p.182
24. Anne Brontë, *Agnes Grey*, Penguin Classics, London, 1988, p.20
25. *Ibid*, pp.46–47
26. *Ibid*, p.92
27. *Ibid*, p.110
28. Anne Brontë, *The Tenant of Wildfell Hall*, Penguin Classics, London, 1996, p.18
29. *Ibid*, p.212
30. Barbara T. Gates, 'Natural History', in Marianne Thormählen (ed), *The Brontës In Context*, Cambridge University Press, 2014, p.257
31. Edward Chitham, *The Poems of Anne Brontë: A New Text and Commentary*, Macmillan Press, London, 1979, p.88
32. Anne Brontë, *Agnes Grey*, Penguin Classics, London, 1988, p.182
33. Anne Brontë, *The Tenant of Wildfell Hall*, Penguin Classics, London, 1996, p.65
34. Anne Brontë, *Agnes Grey*, Penguin Classics, London, 1988, pp.183–184
35. *Ibid*, p.191

CHAPTER FIVE: ANNE AND RELIGION

1. Charlotte Brontë's 'Biographical Notice of Ellis and Acton Bell', in Emily Brontë, *Wuthering Heights*, Penguin Classics, London, 1985, p.34
2. *Ibid*, p.36
3. Anne Brontë, *Agnes Grey and The Tenant of Wildfell Hall*, Everyman's Library, London, 2012, p.ix
4. John Maynard, 'The Brontës and religion', in Heather Glen (ed), *The Cambridge Companion to The Brontës*, Cambridge University Press, Cambridge, 2002, p.193
5. Elizabeth Gaskell, *The Life of Charlotte Bronte*, Oxford University Press, Oxford, 1996, p.49
6. Winifred Gérin, *Anne Brontë: A Biography*, Allen Lane, London, 1976, p.36
7. Miss Ellen Nussey, 'Reminiscences of Charlotte Brontë', *Brontë Society Transactions*, 2:10, pp.58–83, 1899
8. Edward Chitham, *A Life of Anne Brontë*, Blackwell Publishers, Oxford, 1991, p.27
9. Edward Chitham, *The Poems of Anne Brontë: A New Text and Commentary*, MacMillan Press, London, 1979, pp.84–85
10. Juliet Barker, *The Brontës*, Abacus, London, 2010, p.276
11. *Ibid*, p.328
12. David Jasper, 'Religion', in Heather Glen (ed), *The Cambridge Companion to The Brontës*, Cambridge University Press, Cambridge, 2002, p.219
13. Anne Brontë, *Agnes Grey*, Penguin Classics, London, 1988, p.89
14. Juliet Barker, *The Brontës*, Abacus, London, 2010, p.331
15. *Ibid*, p.327
16. Reverend James La Trobe to William Scruton, 1898: see Juliet Barker, *The Brontës: A Life in Letters*, Little, Brown, London, 2016, pp.54–55
17. Marianne Thormählen, 'Anne Brontë and her Bible', *Brontë Studies*, 37:4, pp.339–344, 2012
18. Edward Chitham, *The Poems of Anne Brontë: A New Text and Commentary*, MacMillan Press, London, 1979, p.90
19. Marianne Thormählen, 'Anne Brontë and her Bible', *Brontë Studies*, 37:4, pp.339–344, 2012
20. Anne Brontë, *The Tenant of Wildfell Hall*, Penguin Classics, London, 1996, pp.177–178
21. *Ibid*, p.518
22. *Ibid*, pp.422–423
23. *Ibid*, p.446
24. *Ibid*, p.447
25. Miriam Allott, *The Brontës: The Critical Heritage*, Routledge, London, 2001, p.265
26. Juliet Barker, *The Brontës*, Abacus, London, 2010, p.685
27. Anne Brontë to the Reverend David Thom of Edge Hill, Liverpool, 30 December 1848: see Juliet Barker, *The Brontës: A Life in Letters*, Little, Brown, London, 2016, pp.220–222

28. Anne Brontë, *Agnes Grey*, Penguin Classics, London, 1988, p.89
29. *Ibid*, pp.89–90
30. *Ibid*, p.91
31. Jennifer M. Stolpa, 'Preaching to the clergy: Anne Brontë's Agnes Grey as a treatise on sermon style and delivery', *Victorian Literature and Culture*, 31:1, pp.225–240, 2003
32. *Ibid*
33. Charlotte Brontë's 'Biographical Notice of Ellis and Acton Bell', in Emily Brontë, *Wuthering Heights*, Penguin Classics, London, 1985, p.34

CHAPTER SIX: ANNE'S SOCIAL CONSCIENCE

1. Anne Brontë to Ellen Nussey, 5 April 1849: see Juliet Barker, *The Brontës: A Life in Letters*, Little, Brown, London, 2016, pp.228–229
2. Anne Brontë, *The Tenant of Wildfell Hall*, Penguin Classics, London, 1996, p.4
3. Juliet Barker, *The Brontës*, Abacus, London, 2010, p.308
4. Anne Brontë, *The Tenant of Wildfell Hall*, Penguin Classics, London, 1996, pp.4–5
5. Juliet Barker, *The Brontës*, Abacus, London, 2010, p.1010
6. Emily and Anne's Diary Paper, 24 November 1834, and Emily's Diary Paper, 31 July 1845: see Christine Alexander, *The Brontës: Tales of Glass Town, Angria and Gondal*, Oxford University Press, Oxford, 2010, p.485 and p.491
7. Anne Brontë, *Agnes Grey*, Penguin Classics, London, 1988, p.65
8. *Ibid*, p.64
9. *Ibid*
10. *Ibid*
11. Charlotte Gordon, *Romantic Outlaws: The Extraordinary Lives of Mary Wollstonecraft and Mary Shelley*, Windmill Books, London, 2016, pp.89–90
12. Mary Wollstonecraft, *A Vindication of the Rights of Woman*, Penguin Books, London, 2004, p.129
13. Anne Brontë, *Agnes Grey*, Penguin Classics, London, 1988, p.65
14. *Ibid*
15. *Ibid*, p.66
16. Anne Brontë, *The Tenant of Wildfell Hall*, Penguin Classics, London, 1996, p.34
17. Michael Baggs, 'Gillette faces backlash and boycott over "#MeToo advert"', BBC News, 15 January 2019
18. Anne Brontë, *The Tenant of Wildfell Hall*, Penguin Classics, London, 1996, p.31
19. *Ibid*, p.350
20. Anne Brontë, *Agnes Grey*, Penguin Classics, London, 1988, p.44
21. *Ibid*
22. *Ibid*, p.47
23. Robert Webb, *How Not To Be A Boy*, Canongate Books, London, 2017
24. Anne Brontë, *The Tenant of Wildfell Hall*, Penguin Classics, London, 1996,

p.57
25. Chimamanda Ngozi Adichie, *We Should All Be Feminists*, Fourth Estate, London, 2014, p.37
26. Anne Brontë, *The Tenant of Wildfell Hall*, Penguin Classics, London, 1996, pp.57–58
27. *Ibid*, p.58
28. *Ibid*
29. *Ibid*, p.208
30. Melanie Hamlett, 'Men Have No Friends and Women Bear the Burden', *Harper's Bazaar*, 2 May 2019
31. Anne Brontë, *The Tenant of Wildfell Hall*, Penguin Classics, London, 1996, p.176
32. Anne Brontë, *Agnes Grey*, Penguin Classics, London, 1988, p.114
33. Anne Brontë, *The Tenant of Wildfell Hall*, Penguin Classics, London, 1996, p.201
34. Elizabeth Langland, 'Careers for middle-class women', in Marianne Thormählen (ed), *The Brontës in Context*, Cambridge University Press, 2014, p.303
35. Charlotte Brontë to Ellen Nussey, 10 December 1848: see Juliet Barker, *The Brontës: A Life in Letters*, Little, Brown, London, 2016, p.215
36. Anne Brontë, *Agnes Grey*, Penguin Classics, London, 1988, p.179
37. Edward Chitham, *The Poems of Anne Brontë: A New Text and Commentary*, MacMillan Press, London, 1979, p.14
38. Charlotte Gordon, *Romantic Outlaws: The Extraordinary Lives of Mary Wollstonecraft and Mary Shelley*, Windmill Books, London, 2016, pp.95–96
39. Charlotte Brontë's 'Biographical Notice of Ellis and Acton Bell', in Emily Brontë, *Wuthering Heights*, Penguin Classics, London, 1985, p.31
40. Anne Brontë, *The Tenant of Wildfell Hall*, Penguin Classics, London, 1996, p.5
41. May Sinclair, *The Three Brontës*, Project Gutenberg, 2004
42. Anne Brontë, *The Tenant of Wildfell Hall*, Penguin Classics, London, 1996, p.210
43. Ian Ward, 'Law', in Marianne Thormählen (ed), *The Brontës in Context*, Cambridge University Press, 2014, p.291
44. Anne Brontë, *The Tenant of Wildfell Hall*, Penguin Classics, London, 1996, p.306
45. Marianne Thormählen, 'Marriage and family life', in Marianne Thormählen (ed), *The Brontës in Context*, Cambridge University Press, 2014, p.312
46. Anne Brontë, *The Tenant of Wildfell Hall*, Penguin Classics, London, 1996, p.374
47. *Ibid*, p.262
48. *Ibid*, p.225
49. *Ibid*, p.355
50. *Ibid*, p.358

CHAPTER SEVEN: READING LIKE A BRONTË

1. Juliet Barker, *The Brontës*, Abacus, London, 2010, p.169
2. Christine Alexander, *The Brontës: Tales of Glass Town, Angria and Gondal*, Oxford University Press, Oxford, 2010, p.494
3. Juliet Barker, *The Brontës*, Abacus, London, 2010 p.171
4. Charlotte Brontë, *Jane Eyre*, Penguin Classics, London, 2006, p.11
5. *Ibid*, p.38
6. Charlotte Brontë, *Shirley*, The Folio Society, London, 1968, p.294
7. Edward Chitham, *The Poems of Anne Brontë: A New Text and Commentary*, MacMillan Press, London, 1979, pp.161–162
8. *Ibid*, p.114
9. John Milton, *Paradise Lost*, Oxford University Press, Oxford, 2015, p.1
10. Charlotte Brontë, *Jane Eyre*, Penguin Classics, London, 2006, p.138
11. John Milton, *Paradise Lost*, Oxford University Press, Oxford, 2015 p.64
12. Emily Brontë, *Wuthering Heights*, Penguin Classics, London, 1985, p.122
13. Winifred Gérin, *Emily Brontë: A Biography*, Clarendon Press, Oxford, 1971, p.38
14. Juliet Barker, *The Brontës: A Life In Letters*, Little Brown, London, 2016, pp.47–48
15. *Ibid*, pp.28–29
16. Juliet Barker, *The Brontës*, Abacus, London, 2010, p.319
17. Anne Brontë, *The Tenant of Wildfell Hall*, Penguin Classics, London, 1996, p.73
18. Christine Alexander, *The Brontës: Tales of Glass Town, Angria and Gondal*, Oxford University Press, Oxford, 2010, p.38

AFTERWORD

1. Bill Gibb, 'Scots national poet Jackie Kay hails Anne Brontë in memorial to literary sisters', *Sunday Post*, 19 June 2018

SELECTED BIBLIOGRAPHY

Christine Alexander (ed.), *The Brontës: Tales of Glass Town, Angria and Gondal* (Oxford: Oxford University Press, 2010)

Miriam Allott (ed.), *The Brontës: The Critical Heritage* (London: Routledge, 1974)

Juliet Barker (ed.), *Selected Poems: The Brontës* (London: Everyman, 1993)

Juliet Barker, *The Brontës* (London: Abacus, 2010)

Juliet Barker, *The Brontës: A Life in Letters* (London: Little, Brown, 2016)

Anne Brontë, *Agnes Grey*, ed. Angeline Goreau (London: Penguin Classics, 1988)

Anne Brontë, *The Tenant of Wildfell Hall*, ed. Stevie Davies (London: Penguin Classics, 1996)

Edward Chitham (ed.), *The Poems of Anne Brontë*: A New Text and Commentary (London: MacMillan Press, 1979)

Edward Chitham, *A Life of Anne Brontë* (Oxford: Blackwell Publishers, 1993)

Daphne du Maurier, *The Infernal World of Branwell Brontë* (London: Victor Gollancz, 1960)

Samantha Ellis, *Take Courage: Anne Brontë and the Art of Life* (London: Chatto & Windus, 2017)

Elizabeth Gaskell, *The Life of Charlotte Brontë* (Oxford: Oxford University Press, 1996)

Winifred Gérin, *Anne Brontë: A Biography* (London: Allen Lane, 1976)

Heather Glen (ed.), *The Cambridge Companion to The Brontës* (Cambridge: Cambridge University Press, 2002)

Lucasta Miller, *The Brontë Myth* (New York: Anchor Books, 2005)

Marianne Thormählen (ed.), *The Brontës in Context* (Cambridge: Cambridge University Press, 2014)

INDEX

ACKNOWLEDGEMENTS

I'm very grateful to Sara Hunt and Craig Hillsley at Saraband for their encouragement and support throughout the project, and for making a potentially difficult task feel fun and exciting. Craig's editing skills, in particular, have been invaluable. Thanks also to Alexandra Finch for proofreading and providing the index. Special thanks must go to Claire O'Callaghan, for inspiring me to get started, for her enthusiasm and knowledge about all things Brontë, and her kindness. Thank you to all my friends and family for the love and support: Keri, Ruchi, Jess and Ben, and Chandrika, Tom and Joe – thank you for the confidence!

CHARLOTTE BRONTË REVISITED

World-famous for her novel *Jane Eyre*, Charlotte Brontë is a giant of literature and has been written about in reverential tones in scores of textbooks over the years. But what do we really know about Charlotte? *Sophie Franklin*

EMILY BRONTË REAPPRAISED

Emily Brontë occupies a special place in the English literary canon. And rightly so: the incomparable *Wuthering Heights* is a novel that has bewitched us for almost 200 years. Emily herself remains an enigmatic figure, often portrayed as awkward, as a misanthrope, as "no normal being". That's the conventional wisdom on Emily as a person, but is it accurate, is it fair? *Claire O'Callaghan*